The Pocket Scroll Series

SHAAR PRESS

The Sur

Coping, Persevering, and Winning in Troubled Economic Times

A
SHAAR
PRESS
PUBLICATION

Will Shine Again

Again

Rabbi Abraham J. Twerski, M.D.

TABLE OF CONTENTS

PROLOGUE

"G*algal hu shechozer ba'olam* — the world is repeatedly cyclical" (*Shabbos* 151b).

This principle is as immutable as the law of gravity. This is how Hashem has designed the world. The law of gravity operates by the will of Hashem, as does the cyclical nature of the world. Only under unique circumstances does Hashem suspend His laws, and even then, miracles have been programmed into the design of the world. The Midrash says that at the time of Creation, the dividing of the Reed Sea for the Jews of the Exodus was stipulated (*Shemos Rabbah* 21:6).

The *mefarshim* (commentators) say that the reason the Jewish calendar is based on the moon rather than on the sun is because the cycles of the moon are clearly evident. Its brightness gradually increases, then it dims into total darkness, only to appear again as a glowing celestial light. In the Sanctification of the Moon Service we say, "[The moon] should renew itself as a crown of splendor for those … who are destined to renew themselves like it."

We are in the trough of a cycle. No individual has been singled out. In the chapter on *yissurim* (suffering), I cite the teachings of the sages of *mussar* (ethics), stating that when adversity occurs, we should look at it as a message of guidance for the future rather than as a punishment. It is, of course, extremely distressful to suddenly have the props pulled from beneath one's feet, but one must always remember that there is always renewal, and that he will see the brightness once again.

Adam was created on Friday. The Midrash says that the night of the first Shabbos was bright as day, and the first time Adam experienced darkness was Saturday night. "Woe is me!" Adam said. "My sin has caused light to disappear." When the sun rose on Sunday morning, he was reassured, understanding that this natural cycle is how the world operates.

We should not see the current darkness as doom. The cycle will pass and the sun will shine again.

1. Keeping One's Equilibrium

What is there that one can say? One's job was lost, one's savings were wiped out, the money one put away over many years for one's retirement has gone up in smoke, the money for the children's education has gone, the hopes and dreams for the future have faded into nothingness. Educational and benevolent institutions are losing their support, with teachers and staff losing their jobs. What can anyone say?

When Job was struck by horrendous calamities, three of his friends tried to console him by explaining what had happened, but their unwise words only aggravated his agony. It is foolish to try to explain the unexplainable. Furthermore, if one has slipped on the ice and broken a limb, the pain is not reduced by the understanding that the injury was caused by slipping on the ice.

Is there any validity to the popular adage, *tzaros rabbim chatzi nechamah* (distress shared by others is a partial consolation)? The Talmud relates that when R' Yohanan ben Zakkai's son died, his disciples tried to console him by telling him that Adam, Job, Aaron, and David had lost children, yet they survived and functioned. R' Yohanan said, "Isn't my distress enough? Must you add to it the distress of Adam, Job, Aaron, and David?" (*Avos D'Rebbe Nassan* 14:6). The knowledge that others, too, are suffering gives one scant comfort. Indeed, one suffers additional agony over the plight of others, especially close friends.

But if one remains silent, might it not be assumed that no one cares? One then feels alone in his suffering.

On Tishah B'Av (the fast of the Ninth of Av) we read *Lamentations*, which begins, "Alas! She [Zion] sits in solitude." Bearing one's pain alone may increase its severity.

If only there were magic words that could soothe one's pain!

My Zeide Reb Motele had a heart condition, and he developed a hiccup that lasted several days and was resistant to the usual home remedies. He was taken to a neurology professor in Kiev. The professor felt that the only effective treatment was to shock the spinal cord, which may break the spasm cycle.

Zeide Reb Motele stripped to the waist, and the professor heated an iron poker until it was glowing hot, and ran it down the spinal column. Zeide Reb Motele did not flinch or utter a sound. The professor could not understand this stoicism and repeated the procedure. When there was again no reaction, the professor exclaimed, "I can't believe I am treating a human being! This is some kind of angel. Why, a while back I had a husky Cossack come to me for the treatment, and when I went to get the poker, he jumped out the window. Here I have seared this man twice, and he does not even utter a sound!"

Zeide Reb Motele asked his gabbai (aide) to translate the professor's comment. The gabbai repeated what the professor had said about the Cossack who had escaped through the window even before the poker had been withdrawn from the fire.

Zeide Reb Motele replied, "There are times when a person comes to me and tells me of his tzaros [troubles], but there is nothing I can do to help him. If the pain and anguish I experience at my inability to offer succor doesn't cause me to jump out the window then, I certainly don't have to do so now."

To stand helpless when others suffer is extremely painful.

But if there were really nothing to say, why would you have picked up this book? Obviously, you have some hope that even if there is nothing that can reduce the pain, perhaps there may be some suggestions about what one might do under these excruciating circumstances.

This is certainly not a time to sermonize.

It is related that a famous Torah scholar (some say it was the gaon, Rav Zvi Chayes) was a well-to-do merchant. One time, while he was delivering a shiur (lecture) on Talmud, he received a message that his ship, laden with merchandise, had encountered a storm and had been sunk. This resulted in a great monetary loss, and the gaon fainted.

When he was revived, his students asked him, "Rebbe, you taught us the Gemara that states: A person must praise Hashem for the bad things that happen as well as for the good."

The gaon answered, "I always understood that Gemara al pi drash [in theory], but not al pi peshat [in actuality]." Today's distress is very much al pi peshat, excruciatingly palpable.

One suggestion is that although one may indeed have experienced a disastrous loss, he must take care not to panic. Good judgment must be exercised when making necessary adjustments due to a change in economic status, and when one panics, his judgment will invariably be impaired.

R' Chaim Shmulevitz cites the Talmudic observation that the way the *yetzer hara* (evil inclination) operates is to urge a person to commit a minor transgression, perhaps to deviate from or to ignore the practice of a *minhag* (tradition). After that, it seduces one to commit a more substantial sin, and pursues this gradual downward spiral until it causes one to commit a very serious sin. The *yetzer hara* would hardly have the audacity to tell a *tzaddik* (righteous person) to eat *tereifah* (non-kosher) food. How was it possible then, that the Israelites who had witnessed the revelation at Sinai and who had reached an astonishingly highest level of spirituality were able within a few weeks to have so precipitous a fall as to worship the Golden Calf?

R' Shmulevitz explains that the gradually escalating sequence of sins occurs when a person is emotionally unstable. When the Israelites realized that Moses had not returned by the time they expected him, they assumed that he had died, since it was logical to conclude that no human being could have survived for 40 days without food and water. With Moses gone, they assumed that they were trapped in the arid wilderness, leaderless. At their wits' end and bewildered, they panicked. In a state of panic, anything can happen. Overwhelmed, one may proceed to perform bizarre behavior that would never have been considered under normal circumstances. In a state of panic, they precipitously toppled from the loftiest spiritual heights to the decadence of idolatry.

Despite what has occurred, it is urgent that we keep our wits intact.

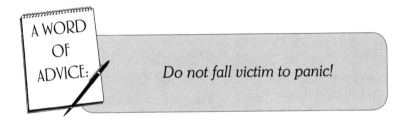

A WORD OF ADVICE: *Do not fall victim to panic!*

2. Maintain a Proper Perspective

The great physician, Sir William Osler, said the words that helped him lead a life free of worry were, "Our main business is not to see what lies dimly at a distance, but to do what lies clearly at hand." Actually, the Talmud had stated this many years before Sir William: "A wise man is superior to a prophet" (*Bava Basra* 12a). That is, a prophet views the future, whereas a wise man deals with the present.

This does not mean that one should not plan for the future. However, when one experiences an adversity such as has resulted from the current economic crisis, one may be so overwhelmed by what the future holds that he may not deal effectively with the present. We should remember that our ancestors in the wilderness were the recipients of the manna, a food allotment that was sufficient for only one day, to teach them not to worry about whether there would be manna tomorrow.

We've already mentioned that in a state of panic, one may do outlandish things. But even when one does not panic, the depressed mood alone can distort his perception.

Almost nothing impacts on a person's self-worth as strongly as the inability to provide adequately for one's family. While that is indeed the way one *may* feel, it is not necessarily the way one *should* feel. A husband is first and foremost a husband, a wife is first and foremost a wife, and parents are first and foremost parents. Children may see their parents differently than the parents see themselves.

The child's mind has not been distorted by the culture's emphasis on money. To her, Dad is Dad and Mom is Mom whether or not he or she has a job. That is how one should feel about himself. One's economic condition is indeed very important, but one's value as a person should not be affected by economics.

Many parents are so preoccupied with earning a livelihood that they do not have adequate time to spend with their children. While children do have needs that can only be met monetarily, their need for parents who love them, care for them, and take a sincere interest in them is more important than the needs satisfied with money. When parents are so occupied with earning money that they cannot devote time to the children, they are making the statement, "Giving you things is more important than giving you myself." Children do not see things this way unless we convince them that this is so.

I must go back to my emphasis on self-esteem, which is based on a comment by R' Yitzchak Meir of Gur. The spies that Moses sent to scout Canaan returned with a report that the land was inhabited by a race of giants. "All the people that we saw in it were huge! There we saw the Nephilim, the sons of the giant from among the Nephilim; *we were like grasshoppers in our eyes, and so we were in their eyes!*" (emphasis added) (*Numbers* 13:32-33). "The Torah is telling us," said R' Yitzchak Meir, "that the way we feel about ourselves is the way we think other people feel about us." In addition, the way we feel about ourselves may cause others to perceive us in the same way.

Children, certainly small children, see their parents as wise and powerful. Their parents are their primary source of security. They need their parents' embrace. Their minds have not been contaminated by the prevailing worship of finances. However, if the parents' self-esteem is so low that they consider themselves to be only a meal ticket, they will think that this is the children's opinion of them and fail to realize how much they mean to the children.

One mother said, "I have given myself totally to my children. But then what have they gotten? Nothing!" If a parent thinks of oneself as nothing, then one feels that the children receive nothing other than whatever is purchased for them.

As long as parents feel they are able to provide adequately for their children, they may not be tormented by such feelings. However, if they suffer a financial reversal, and they do not have a positive sense of self-worth, they may become very depressed. This depression can be addressed psychologically.

One man said, "My daughter is engaged. When we met the *mechutanim* [in-laws], I made a commitment to make a beautiful wedding and to support the couple for several years. But I was wiped out and I cannot live up to my pledge. What can I do?"

If one is depressed, one might try to avoid talking to the *mechutanim*, as if avoiding the problem will set it straight. If one keeps his bearings, he should meet with the *mechutanim* and explain the situation to them. If they are *mentschen* (decent human beings), they will certainly not fault parents for something beyond their control. They will understand that a solid marriage need not be founded on monetary matters and that the children can be happily married. Obviously, the plans will have to be rethought as to how the young couple will live under these altered conditions.

We are in a situation of a *tzaros rabbim,* a crisis that affects many people, and it is unimaginable that people will not empathize. If the *mechutanim* should take an attitude, "Your tough luck. No money, no *shidduch* [match]," the parents can try to have a Rav reason with them. If they are intractable and break the *shidduch,* it is indeed most unfortunate. However, why would someone wish to marry into a family in which the parents are not *mentschen*?

This is a time when everyone needs *chizuk* (moral support). Husbands and wives should be supportive of each other. Rebbeim in yeshivos and teachers in girls' schools should discuss the present economic situation with students, make them aware of their parents' predicament, and teach them how important it is to be supportive. Children should understand that although this economic crisis was beyond the parents' control, the parents may nevertheless feel that they have let their children down, and they should show their parents how much they respect and appreciate them.

Small children are exquisitely sensitive, and they may pick up on their parents' anxiety. Because they are not aware of Wall Street and layoffs, their imagination can run wild. We have no idea what they may fear. It is important to increase the amount of time spent with the children, to tell reassuring stories (not the horrors of *Grimm's Fairy Tales*). The kids need lots of hugs. Sometimes children who have long slept in a darkened room may want a night-light again. There may be recurrence of bedwetting or thumb-sucking. They may regress to baby talk or to throwing tantrums. Their school performance may be affected. When you leave the house, even to go shopping, they may be worried. Reassure them, "Mommy is just going to the store. I'll be right back."

Children often take words literally. If there is talk about someone who was fired from his job, the child may take the word "fire" literally and assume that he was burned. One crying child said, "I'm afraid they're going to burn Daddy."

Children may ask, "What's wrong?" Saying, "Nothing's wrong. Everything is okay," will not reassure them. Their parents may be tense and irritable, and the children sense this. They will feel they are being lied to and their imagination will run wild. They will assume that what happened is so horrific that their parents cannot even talk about it. While they may not be able to understand that there is a national economic crisis, you can tell them that many people are having a hard time because they are out of work, but that things will eventually get better. They may not understand completely, but they will feel you are telling them the truth, and that is reassuring.

Find some time to play games with the children. It will do them a great deal of good, and will do even more good for you.

One man said, "My older two daughters attended seminary

in Israel. My youngest daughter will be graduating high school and has her heart set on going to Israel like her sisters did, but I lost my job and a great deal of money. I just can't afford it. Several of her friends will be going to study in Israel, however, and will be showing her what they bought for the year there. How do I tell her that she cannot go to Israel? What will this do to her?"

Our job as parents is to prepare our children to live in the real world, and in the real world there are often disappointments. A high-school senior is not unaware of the economic crisis, and she should be told the facts. The parents must empathize with her and understand her pain. Saying something on the order of, "The seminaries here are just as good," would be ignoring her feelings. Regardless of the relative merits of the seminaries, her disappointment in losing the experience of a year in Israel would still be profound. She should be helped to understand that the whole family must pull together to survive the current crisis as best as they can.

If the father feels that because he is unable to send his daughter to a seminary in Israel he is a failure, this may cause her to feel guilty for making the father feel this way. The father's depression may then have a ripple effect, adding unwarranted guilt feelings to her disappointment.

In some cases, a couple's *shalom bayis* (marital harmony) may be fragile, and they are barely managing to preserve the marriage, perhaps for the children's sake. They may not have sought counseling to repair the *shalom bayis*, but are just limping along on their own. If the family income is seriously compromised, this adds a significant stress, with everyone suffering disappointment, and under these circumstances, a weak marriage may collapse. The financial pressures may cause spouses to be irritable, and annoyances that would otherwise be overlooked may take on huge proportions.

It should be evident that the loss of income due to the economic crisis is not the fault of either spouse. If this calamity results in the couple considering themselves incompatible, it may indicate that other reasons for the couple's *shalom bayis* problems may also not be as valid as they may appear. Rather than dissolve the marriage because of the added economic stress, the couple should consult a professional with competence in marriage counseling, and the underlying *shalom bayis* issues that had not been addressed may actually be resolved.

The Talmud is well aware of the stress that financial worries can place on a marriage (*Bava Metzia* 59a), stating that a husband should be particularly respectful to his wife because "the blessing of the household is by virtue of the wife." Rava told his community, "Honor your wives so that you should achieve success" (ibid.). Think of how you would jump at the opportunity if your broker told you that a particular stock would go up considerably in value. When you enhance your *shalom bayis* by being considerate of your wife, the Talmud promises you success.

———————

Just as it is a mistake to be overwhelmed by the prospects of the future, it is equally wrong to be overwhelmed by the past. All the "I should have" thoughts are worse than worthless, not only because one cannot undo the past, but because preoccupation with the past precludes concentrating on the present. One should learn from one's mistakes, determine not to repeat them, but then let go of them.

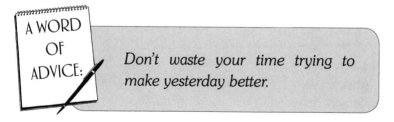

A WORD OF ADVICE:

Don't waste your time trying to make yesterday better.

3. DEPRESSION WITHOUT DESPAIR

It would be foolish to minimize the severe blows that many people have sustained. It has been said in jest that the difference between a recession and a depression is that when others lose their jobs, it is a recession, but when I lose my job, it is a depression. However, depression should not lead to hopelessness.

Some people may say that a firm faith in Hashem should prevent depression. That, too, is foolish. We can rest assured that someone of the stature of the Rambam has a deep and abiding faith in Hashem. Rambam was able to devote himself entirely to Torah study and to the composition of his great works, which are the pillars of Jewish law and thought, because he was supported by his younger brother, David, a diamond merchant. Catastrophe struck when David drowned at sea, his fortune going down with him. Not only was Rambam now destitute, but he also had to provide for David's widow and children.

Rambam went into a deep depression. "I was at death's door," he said. Even years later, he was grieving. "Years have waned, but I still mourn and find no solace. And what could possibly bring me solace? He [David] grew up on my lap. He was my brother and my pupil. He had a business and earned a livelihood for us both, and I could live without care. He was conversant with the Talmud and knew the grammar of the Hebrew language. My only joy was to see him. All my joy is gone. He has passed on to eternal life, leaving me shattered in a strange land. Whenever I see his handwriting or one of his books, my heart turns over, and my grief is roused once again. 'Had Your Torah not been my preoccupation, then I would perish in my affliction'" (Psalms 119:92).

Rambam does not say that his devotion to Torah prevented him from being depressed. What Torah did for him was *prevent despair*, prevent his perishing, and allow him to function even when depressed. Rambam continued producing his epochal Torah writings as well a number of medical works. He was not a businessman but became a doctor, serving as court physician to the son of the sultan.

> The Talmud relates that King Hezekiah was ill, and the prophet Isaiah came to visit him. "I have sad tidings for you," Isaiah said. "I have received a prophecy that your death is imminent."
>
> "Take your prophecy and leave," King Hezekiah said. "We have a tradition from King David that even if the sword is at one's throat, one should not despair of Divine mercy." King Hezekiah prayed to G-d, and his life was extended for many years (Berachos 10a).

This is a fundamental principle of Torah. There is never any justification for despair. R' Nachman of Breslov said, "In reality, there is no such thing as despair. A person who feels hopeless is delusional. Despair simply does not exist."

Genesis 21:14-19 relates that Hagar was wandering in the desert with her son, Ishmael, and they ran out of water. She cast Ishmael under a tree and sat afar because she could not watch Ishmael die. An angel appeared to her and told her that Ishmael would live. "Then G-d opened her eyes and she perceived a well of water ...." There was no miraculous creation of a well. The well was always there, but in her despair, she did not see it.

That is what may happen when a person loses hope. There may be a solution to one's problem, but in a state of despair, one cannot see it.

R' Nachman's statement is intriguing. What does he mean by saying that despair does not exist? A person who feels there is no hope is in a state of despair. How can he say that despair does not exist?

But R' Nachman is right. A paranoid person may hear voices, and to him, these voices are very real. He does, in fact, hear them. However, these voices do not exist in reality. They are not broadcast to him through the airwaves; they are not heard by a physical ear. Yet although they do not exist in reality, there is no way one can convince a paranoid that these voices are not real. To him they are very real, although they are a hallucination, and his belief that the voices are real is a delusion.

This is similar to the case of the feeling of despair. There is no denying that a person can feel hopeless. However, just as the feeling of hearing voices is delusional, so is the feeling of hopelessness delusional. Inasmuch as the person who feels despair is not mentally ill, he should be able to realize that he is feeling something that does not exist, just as the voices heard by the paranoid do not exist in reality.

What could be more certain than a prophecy, a message from Hashem? Yet King Hezekiah said that even then there is hope.

The psalmist says "Hope to Hashem, be strong and strengthen your heart, and hope to Hashem" (*Psalms* 27:14). Why the repetition? Because it may be difficult to hope, and one may have to gather strength in order to be able to hope. If one finds that he cannot hope, he must try to strengthen himself so that he will be able to hope.

> Let me share a first-person story with you. During World War II, a family that belonged to my father's congregation was notified that their son was missing in action in the European theater of war. Understandably, they were devastated. My father tried to give them hope, to lift their spirits by telling them that missing-in-action status does not mean that he had been killed. He suggested that the son was probably a prisoner of war and would return when the war was over. Once a week, my father would visit the family to keep up their hopes that their son was alive.
>
> When the war was over, it was found that, indeed, their son had been a prisoner of war. The son returned to his base before going home, and found a stack of letters that my father had written to him. These were written before each weekly visit to the parents' home. My father had to reinforce his own hope that the son was alive, in order to be effective in conveying hope to the parents. That was his way of fulfilling the verse, "… be strong and strengthen your heart."

I know that it is difficult to muster hope when one has suffered severe adversity. I don't expect that by receiving *chizuk* from people or from *sefarim* (books on religious topics) one will be happy and will begin dancing joyously. Few people have achieved that high a spiritual level. But these sources of *chizuk* should enable one to hold onto hope and to allow a glimmer of light to penetrate the darkness.

When Jacob was fleeing from Esau, he said, "… whence will come my help? My help is from Hashem, Maker of heaven and earth" (*Psalms* 121:1-2). Just as Hashem made heaven and earth out of nothingness, so can He deliver a person's salvation when one sees no source of help.

When our ancestors stood at the Reed Sea with Pharaoh's army pursuing them, no one thought that they would be saved by the sea splitting before them. There are many instances of people who emerged from what appeared to be impossible circumstances. It has been said, "In times like these, it helps to recall that there have always been times like these." Let us remember that adversity is an experience, not a final act.

I attended a meeting of recovering alcoholics; it was a "gratitude meeting," at which each person expressed his or her gratitude for having been given a second chance in life, and how good things were now. One person arose and said, "I have been sober for four years, and I wish I could tell you that things have been good. My company downsized, I lost my job and haven't been able to find another job. My wife divorced me and took custody of the children. I was unable to pay the mortgage, and they foreclosed on my house. Last week the finance company repossessed my car. But I can't believe that G-d brought me all this way just to walk out on me now. I know that He has a plan for me and that one day, things will be good."

The following Shabbos, as I said *Nishmas*, I truly heard for the first time what I had been saying for many years. "Hashem, You took us out of Egypt and delivered us from enslavement. In famine You nourished us, and in plenty You provided for us. You rescued us from the sword, and saved us from epidemics and from serious diseases. Until now Your compassion has helped us and Your mercies have not forsaken us, *and You will not abandon us unto eternity*." Hashem did not bring us all this way only to walk out on us now. He will help us in the future as He did in the past.

I still have hope that one day I might become wise. Inasmuch as the Talmud says, "Who is wise? He who learns from every person" (*Ethics of the Fathers* 4:1), I make an effort to learn from everyone. I learned something more from yet another recovered alcoholic.

The recovery program requires that a person "turn over one's will to the will of G-d." This concept preceded the recovery program by two thousand years. The Talmud says, "Make His will your will" (ibid. 2:4), but I heard this thesis presented in a rather unique way by a recovered alcoholic.

"I am a rabid football fan," this man said. "The New York Jets are my team, and I never miss a game. One weekend I had to be away, so I asked a friend to record the game for me on his VCR. When I returned and picked up the videotape, my friend said, 'By the way, the Jets won.'

"I started watching the game, and horrors! The Jets were playing terribly. At halftime, they were 20 points behind. Under other circumstances, I would have been a nervous wreck: my team was losing so badly. But I wasn't nervous at all. I was perfectly calm, because I knew that they were going to win.

"Things don't always go smoothly for me. But when I entered the recovery program, I made a conscious decision to turn my will over to the will of G-d. I know that eventually it will turn out all right. There are times when I'm '20 points behind at halftime,' but I'm not shaken by that. I can't be sure that *my* will will make things turn out okay, but *His* will will do it."

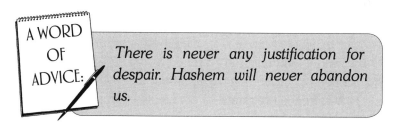

A WORD OF ADVICE:

There is never any justification for despair. Hashem will never abandon us.

4. GETTING UP WHEN YOU'RE DOWN

Several years ago, I wrote *Getting Up When You're Down*, a book that dealt with various types of depression and their related symptoms. That book warranted a psychiatric approach, because it discusses conditions that are deviations from the normal, whether these are due to biochemical changes in the body or to experiences that resulted in a distortion of emotions. These are conditions that can be relieved by appropriate medications or psychological treatment.

However, the problems we are facing today are hardly of a psychiatric nature; they are firmly rooted in reality. Reacting with anxiety, depression, and insomnia to the loss of employment, life's savings, and retirement plans, the sudden eradication of one's hopes and dreams is not abnormal. What can I, as a psychiatrist, possibly offer? All the Prozac in the world will not restore the lost job or life's savings.

As a psychiatrist, let me first tell you what *not* to do. Insomnia and anxiety are very distressing, and one may resort to sedatives for a night's sleep or to an occasional tranquilizer to settle one's nerves. Proceed with caution! All substances of this ilk, if used with regularity, eventually lose their effectiveness, and if one becomes dependent on them, one may use increasing amounts to get some respite. This can result in very serious addictions that may be difficult to overcome.

Similarly, if one relies on alcohol to put one into a stupor in order to get to sleep, one is at risk of developing addiction to alcohol. Neither alcohol, nor tranquilizers, nor sleeping pills will restore the lost job or savings. They may make one temporarily forget what has happened by dulling the sensitivity of the brain. By the same token, they decrease the brain's ability to make an optimal adjustment to a difficult situation and they fog the mind, preventing one from arriving at productive solutions. If a person resorts to these soporifics to deal with a financial loss, one may end up with a financial loss *plus* a serious addiction problem.

Insomnia, as distressing as it may be, has never killed anyone. Addiction to sedatives has killed many people.

Nevertheless, while it is true that no one has ever died of insomnia, a person *can* become ill by *worrying* about insomnia. The common-sense methods of exercise, practicing meditation, and expressing trust in Hashem by reading the *Shema* (especially the complete Bedtime *Shema* that can be found in comprehensive *siddurim* and in the ArtScroll booklet) can help one get to sleep. One man said, "My worries kept me awake. Then I realized that Hashem is always awake. There's no purpose in both of us being up."

No, it is not abnormal to feel depressed by these losses. However, there may be fallout and ripple effects that are emotional disturbances.

One man stated that he could no longer *daven* (pray) in the *shul* (synagogue) where he had prayed for 20 years. Why? Because, previously, every time he had been called to the Torah, he had pledged $100 to the *shul*, but he could no longer give a donation of this amount and he was embarrassed to be unable to announce his usual pledge.

While I certainly understand this man's feelings, they are really not legitimate. Unfortunately, we may have succumbed to the popular concept, when inquiring about a person's assets, to say, "How much is he worth?" A person's worth should not be determined by how much he owns, and one should not feel any less worth when his fortunes have changed.

Here is something to think about. Make every effort to do

so sincerely and to be utterly honest with yourself.

Yes, you are distressed because you have suffered great losses, but how much of this distress is due to how you have been affected in terms of what you can or cannot afford, and how much is due to what you feel is a devaluation of your public image?

In my writings on self-esteem, I repeatedly point out that we should never permit other people to determine who we are. We should forge our own identity, an identity that should be no different when living in a large city than if we were isolated on an island. If your identity is dependent on what others think of you, then you really have no identity at all, because you must be one thing for this person and something else for that person. Your self-esteem and self-worth are then constantly at the mercy of others.

R' Mendel of Kotzk said, "If I am I because I am I, and you are you because you are you, then I exist and you exist. However, if I am I *because* you are you, and you are you *because* I am I, then I do not exist and you do not exist." In the latter case, one exists only as the product of another person's will.

I suspect that the person who is reluctant to *daven* in his *shul* is really distressed not because he is unable to donate as much as he would like, but because he fears what others will be thinking if he pledges $10 rather than $100.

Attaining an identity of one's own is of prime importance in good times as well as in bad times.

> *Rabbi Chaim Shmulevitz cites the Midrash relating that King Solomon was banished from his throne by Ashmidai, king of the demons. Solomon begged for food from door to door, and when he said, "I am the king," people jeered at him, believing him to be a madman. The Talmud says that initially, Solomon was a powerful monarch, king over a vast empire, the greatest of the great, and when he was dethroned and had to beg for food, he was "king only over his walking stick" (Sanhedrin 20b).*
>
> *Rabbi Shmulevitz says that in the throes of his impoverishment, Solomon was still "king over his walking stick," i.e., he never forgot that he was king. His circumstances were disastrous, but he did not allow them to crush him. He maintained his sense of royalty even when he had to beg for food.*

Heed Rabbi Shmulevitz's words: "*A person must be most cautious when he suffers a fall, not to allow the fall to harm him even more than the actual adverse circumstances. If he will strengthen himself even in his decline and maintain his personal value under all circumstances, there is hope that he will rise and return to his former status and even higher than that*" (*Sichos Mussar* 5731:13).

This is a precious Torah insight. Sometimes we cannot control what happens to us, but we *can* control how we react.

If a Rav or a member of the congregation becomes aware that a regular worshiper is no longer attending *shul*, he should investigate what has happened; if it is discovered that the person is sensitive and feels embarrassed, he should be brought back to the *shul* and reassured that, despite his financial reverses, being a respected member of the *shul* is not contingent on how much he donates.

Whereas depressed feelings due to losses are normal and should not be relieved by antidepressant medication, it is nevertheless possible that the stress of prolonged worrying and insomnia may indeed cause a chemical imbalance, creating a secondary depression that can be helped by medication. If one suffers continued insomnia, loss of appetite, crying, and feelings of despair, one should consult a psychiatrist.

A WORD OF ADVICE: *Do not allow circumstances to overwhelm you. Never resort to alcohol or sedatives to mask your feelings.*

5. I Gave Much
Tzeddakah

There are much greater philanthropists than I am, but I did give significant amounts of money to various institutions," one person told me. "People would come to the morning *minyan* primarily to see me. I would give them $10 or $20 with a smile. I can no longer do that. I apologize to people because I cannot give the way I used to. I'm not asking Hashem for a reward for the *tzeddakah* [charity] I gave. I would just like to not feel bad when I disappoint people by giving them $2 instead of $20."

I shared with the man the well-known Talmudic statement that one who gives less is just as meritorious as one who gives much, as long as the intention is to do Hashem's will. Then I told him the following Talmudic excerpt.

> The great sage, Rabbi Eliezer, fell seriously ill, and his students came to comfort him. R' Tarfon said, "Our master! You are dearer to us than the rain. The rain can provide a person only with this world, but you, our master, have provided us with the World to Come." Rabbi Eliezer remained silent and did not acknowledge him.
>
> R' Yehoshua said, "Our master! You are dearer to us than the orbit of the sun. The sun can provide a person only with this world, but you, our master, have provided us with the World to Come." Again, Rabbi Eliezer remained silent.
>
> R' Elazar ben Azariah addressed him, "Our master! You are dearer to us than a father and mother. A father and mother can provide a child only with this world, but you, our master, have provided us with the World to Come." Rabbi Eliezer did not acknowledge this student's comment either.
>
> Then Rabbi Akiva spoke up. "Suffering can be precious," he said.
>
> Rabbi Eliezer said, "Help me sit up so that I can better hear what my child, Akiva, has to say."

The other students had made comments that should have comforted Rabbi Eliezer. Why did he ignore them and respond only to Rabbi Akiva?

Resting on one's laurels is *gaavah* (vanity; arrogance) and achieves nothing. Rabbi Eliezer valued life because it provided him with the opportunity to do Hashem's will. But he was now weak and bedridden and could do nothing. This depressed him, and the fact that he had achieved much in the past did not comfort him in the least. He could be comforted only if there was something he could do at that time.

Rabbi Akiva's statement implied that Hashem's will is that a person should maximize oneself spiritually. This is what man was created for, and maximizing oneself in the service of Hashem is the only thing that Rabbi Eliezer felt was of value. However, in his condition, he did not see anything he could do that would be spiritually fulfilling.

Rabbi Akiva said that *avodas Hashem* (service of Hashem) consists of doing whatever one can do *at any particular moment, given his condition at that moment.* What he told the master was essentially, "When you had the ability to teach, your *tafkid* [assignment] was teaching. Your present condition does not permit you to teach. All you can do now is to accept your suffering with trust and faith in Hashem's justice, and when you do that, you are fulfilling your *tafkid* every bit as much as when you taught us."

We are obligated to do what our circumstances enable us to do, and this is true of giving *tzeddakah* as well. If his income has been curtailed, he should give *tzeddakah* according to his means. The merit of *tzeddakah* will bring one the *berachah* (blessing) of Hashem.

Like many tzaddikim, R' Meir of Premishlan was lavish in giving tzeddakah. He explained, "After his lifetime, a man approached the Heavenly Tribunal, asking to be admitted to Gan Eden. 'What merits do you have?' he was asked.

"'I davened three times a day,' he said.

"The tribunal responded, 'We have evaluated your davening. You did not daven with kavannah [concentration]. You thought of your business during davening. That does not earn you Gan Eden.'

"'I learned Torah,' the man said.

"The tribunal responded, 'Yes. But your intent in learning Torah was that you wanted people to look up to you as a scholar. That was not the proper intent, and it does not earn you Gan Eden.'

"Then the man said, 'I gave tzeddakah.'

"The doors of Gan Eden were promptly opened for him. 'With tzeddakah,' the tribunal said, 'we don't check into kavannah or intent. As long as the needy person was able to obtain food and clothing and pay his bills, your mitzvah is complete.'

"So," R' Meir said, "I wish to take advantage of a mitzvah that will have merit regardless of how I do it."

Inasmuch as it is a greater sacrifice to give *tzeddakah* when one's income has decreased, the reward for such *tzeddakah* is very great.

Furthermore, *tzeddakah* is an infinite mitzvah.

> *Two cases came before the Heavenly Tribunal. One concerned a man who had given $100 to tzeddakah and the other was regarding a man who had stolen $100. The man who gave tzeddakah received a great reward, whereas the man who stole was given a limited punishment. One of the angels questioned the fairness of these decisions.*
>
> *The tribunal explained, "With this $100, a poor person was able to buy food for his hungry family. Because they were well nourished, the children were healthy, grew, and did mitzvos. The man who gave tzeddakah certainly wanted all these benefits to accrue from his gift, so he is rewarded for the long-range effects of the mitzvah. However, the man who stole the money did so out of desperation because he could not pay his rent. He certainly had no desire for the victim of the theft to suffer. Therefore, even if there were consequences resulting from his sin, he never desired them, so his punishment is limited to the sin itself."*

Although *kavannah* is not essential to *tzeddakah*, the mitzvah increases exponentially when *tzeddakah* is given with consideration for the recipient. The needy person who receives *tzeddakah* is undoubtedly brokenhearted by his plight, and if the *tzeddakah* is given graciously, with a smile, and with the *berachah*, "Hashem should give you *hatzlachah* [success]," the merit is extraordinarily great.

People who have been severely affected by the economic crisis and who may have to deprive themselves of things they had been able to afford previously can more readily empathize with people who are in need.

R' Motele, the Maggid of Chernoble, frequently collected money to ransom Jews who had been imprisoned by the poritz (feudal lord), usually because they were in arrears on their rent. On one occasion, some anti-Semites brought a false accusation of treason against R' Motele, and he was imprisoned.

One of R' Motele's chaverim (peers), R' Zev of Zhitomir, visited him in prison. "Let me tell you why you're here," he said. "Avraham Avinu was hospitable to wayfarers. Hashem said to him, 'What you are doing is indeed great, but you can not do it full-heartedly unless you know what it feels like to be a wayfarer and need food and a place to rest. Therefore, lech lecha [Go for yourself (Genesis 12:1)]; experience personally what it feels like to be away from home and need food and rest. Then you will be able to do the mitzvah in a much better way.'

"So it is with you," R' Zev continued. "You were doing a great mitzvah by redeeming Jews from prison, but now that you have experienced imprisonment yourself, your efforts and motivation will increase greatly."

Although people gave much *tzeddakah* in the past, if they now experience the feeling of deprivation, their *tzeddakah* can take on a different character.

A WORD OF ADVICE:

Dire straits enable us to empathize with others. One's tafkid — doing the will of Hashem — can be fulfilled whatever the circumstances.

6. GREATER THAN TZEDDAKAH?

As we have mentioned, added to the trauma of a financial setback is the distress of not being able to give as much *tzeddakah* as one was accustomed to bestow. The Talmud says, "Even more than the calf wishes to suckle, the cow wishes to nurse" (*Pesachim* 112a). A person may not have been aware of how much he wishes to give *tzeddakah* until the ability to do so was curtailed.

The Talmud says that doing *gemilas chassadim* (acts of kindness) is even greater than giving *tzeddakah*, because *tzeddakah* is done with one's possessions, whereas *gemilas chassadim* is done with one's person. *Tzeddakah* benefits only the poor, whereas *gemilas chassadim* benefits both the rich and the poor. *Tzeddakah* is given only to the living, whereas *gemilas chassadim* applies to both the living and the departed (*Succah* 49b).

Gemilas chassadim is not only greater in the sense that it is more applicable. Maharsha says that *gemilas chassadim* is the greatest of all the mitzvos (ibid.). "One who engages in *gemilas chassadim* is as though he fulfilled the Ten Commandments" (*Midrash Hagadol, Bereishis* 23). "If, when one lies in bed at night, thinks, *When I get up tomorrow I am going to do something good for a person*, he is destined to rejoice with the *tzaddikim* in the World to Come (*Yalkut Shimoni, Mishlei* 12:949).

Just how great a mitzvah *gemilas chassadim* is can be surmised from the priority given to it by our *tzaddikim*.

> *R' Yisrael of Salant, the founder of the mussar movement, was once seen standing in the street and nonchalantly chatting casually with someone. His students were shocked, because they knew that R' Yisrael was totally devoted to Torah study and tefillah, and he never engaged in idle talk. One student was curious enough to mention this to R' Yisrael, who said, "This man is depressed. There can be no gemilas chassadim greater than trying to lift his spirits."*

It is worth repeating the well-known anecdote recounting that one Yom Kippur eve, R' Yisrael was not in shul for Kol Nidrei. Fearing that something untoward might have happened to him, several worshipers went to look for him, but they did not find him. Toward the end of Maariv, R' Yisrael appeared, and davened the Yom Kippur prayers b'yichidus (on his own) rather than with the congregation, which had already finished praying.

After the davening, the congregants learned what had delayed him. On the way to shul, R' Yisrael had passed a house and heard an infant crying inside. He entered the house and saw that an infant was wailing in his crib, with the bottle of milk at his side. A 6-year-old girl was sitting nearby, fast asleep. He understood that the mother had gone to Kol Nidrei and the little girl was supposed to tend to the baby's needs, but had dozed off. R' Yisrael gave the baby the bottle and rocked the cradle until the infant was asleep. The little girl awoke and beseeched him not to leave, because she was afraid to be in the house alone. R' Yisrael waited until the mother returned, and only then proceeded to shul.

———»•«———

One of R' Yisrael's students, a great Talmudical scholar, went into business after his marriage, but his business failed. He would spend time in the beis midrash, discussing Torah with his friends. He once posed a possible elucidation of a difficult passage in the Talmud, which no one else could explain. Just then R' Yisrael walked in, and they told him the problem. R' Yisrael reviewed the portion of the Talmud, and concurred with the explanation, implying that he had not been able to resolve the question himself.

After the young man left, another Rosh Yeshivah privately asked R' Yisrael how it was possible that he hadn't known the resolution of the passage in question. R' Yisrael responded, "The meaning of this Talmud is actually quite simple. But this young man is depressed because of the failure of his business. I reasoned it would lift his spirits if he thought that he had answered a question that had stumped the Rosh Yeshivah."

The gaon R' Aharon Kotler stated that when he stayed late into the night with his rebbi, R' Nosson Tzvi Finkel, the Elder of Slabodka, the latter would escort him to the major intersection near R' Aharon's home. Reb Nosson Tzvi would wait there until he saw R' Aharon enter his house.

A Rav related that as a young man, he went to Radin to join the yeshivah of the Chofetz Chaim. He arrived late at night, went into the beis midrash, and lay down on a bench to sleep. When he awoke, he realized that he was covered with a blanket. The Chofetz Chaim was standing beside him, holding a pan of water and a towel. After he had washed his hands, the Chofetz Chaim gave him a piece of cake and some warm milk. "You must be tired and hungry from your trip," he said.

Imagine the scene: The Chofetz Chaim standing patiently at the boy's bedside, waiting for him to wake up so that he could give him cake and milk!

—————

It was the custom of R' Yehoshua of Belz to walk up and down the aisles of the shul on Yom Kippur afternoon, looking at the faces of the worshipers. The chassidim were sure that the rebbe was looking at them to see if they were doing sincere teshuvah (repentance). The true reason became apparent when R' Yehoshua saw that one man had become deathly ill because he was fasting; the rebbe whipped out a small bottle of brandy and a cookie to revive the person.

—————

In one shul, there was a man who served as chazzan every Rosh Hashanah. When he died, the shul began the search for a new chazzan. The rebbe said that he wanted the chazzan's son to assume his father's position. Some members objected, saying that the young man was not married, and the Shulchan Aruch says that it is preferable that the chazzan be a family man. Furthermore, the son was still in the year of mourning.

"I know," the rebbe said, "but think of how the widow will feel when a stranger provides the services that her husband did. At least, if she hears her son's voice, it will give her some comfort."

———

R' Levi Yitzchak of Berditchev visited a person who was terminally ill and was crying. When R' Levi Yitzchak asked why he was crying, the man said, "I know my end is near, and I have no merits to bring to the Heavenly Tribunal."

R' Levi Yitzchak said, "Have no worry. I am giving you the merits of all the mitzvos I did all my life."

When someone asked R' Levi Yitzchak how he could do such a thing, R' Levi Yitzchak said, "I will gladly give away all my Gan Eden so that a person can have peace of mind."

———

The Chofetz Chaim was invited to someone's home for Shabbos, and accepted the invitation on condition that all the zemiros (Shabbos songs) and divrei Torah (Torah lessons) be postponed until after the last course had been served. After *the meal, the cook came into the dining room and thanked the Chofetz Chaim.*

"Every Friday night I must wait for hours until the meal is over. It is so wonderful to be finished early. Now I can go home and have some Shabbos with my family."

These anecdotes all teach us that *gemilas chassadim* means caring for another person. This does not cost money and need not constitute a major sacrifice. All that is required is that you show a person consideration and that you care. For example, after you have washed your hands for the *seudah* (festive meal) at a wedding, fill the washing cup for the person behind you. (R' Simchah Zissel of Kelm required this of all the yeshivah students.) When you spread rock salt on your icy walk, spread some on your neighbor's walk, too.

If you know of a friend who has suffered from the economic crisis, invite him for a Shabbos meal. This may not compensate for the money lost, but joining you in *zemiros* and camaraderie can help lift his spirits.

I've seen people pass each other on Shabbos without a greeting. Just saying "Good Shabbos" with a smile is *gemilas chassadim*. So is welcoming a newcomer to the *shul*. Handing a person a *siddur* or *Chumash* is *gemilas chassadim*.

Join in your friends' *simchos* (joyous occasions). When my son became a bar mitzvah, I asked a friend why I had not received a reply to the invitation to the celebration. He said, "You would have received one if I had gotten an invitation." I was stymied. I clearly remembered sending him an invitation. I subsequently discovered that many of the people whose last names began with "P" or "R" did not receive invitations. Something must have happened to that group of invitations.

Ever since, if I do not receive an invitation to a friend's wedding or bar mitzvah, I go anyway, because I sincerely want to wish them a "mazal tov" and to dance with them. Inasmuch as they did not reserve a seat for me, I do not stay for the meal, but I want to share my friends' *simchos*.

A WORD OF ADVICE:

It is so easy to fulfill the mitzvah of gemilas chassadim. We need only look for the opportunities and we will find them.

7. Remember the Shabbos to Keep It Holy

I realize that the financial losses one has suffered weigh heavily on his mind, and he thinks of what he can do to better his situation. Even if one is unable to free oneself of these worries during the week, these worries must come to an end when the Shabbos candles are lit. Shabbos is Hashem's special gift to the Jewish people, and it should be celebrated with joy.

Yes, you have always observed Shabbos, but now do something extra. It is a special *segulah* (spiritual cure) to show how dear Shabbos is by assisting in its preparation. Help clean the house for Shabbos. Use the broom, mop, and vacuum cleaner. Do something in the kitchen to assist in preparing the Shabbos food. The Talmud describes how the great sages used to participate in preparing for Shabbos.

A special *segulah* is to have the table set and the Shabbos candles ready before noon on Friday. Let me share with you a story that was related by Rabbi Kaplan of Safed.

As a youngster, Rabbi Kaplan learned in the Mir Yeshivah, and roomed with a family. Every Friday morning, the husband went to the market to buy provisions for Shabbos, and his wife would say, "Come back early." One time, Rabbi Kaplan came to the house on Friday before noon, and saw the wife standing at the window, watching for her husband.

"Why are you so anxious?" the young Rabbi Kaplan asked. "It is early. There is still plenty of time until Shabbos."

"I'll tell you why," she said. "We have only one child, a son who was born many years after we were married. I realized that the child was not developing properly, and when the doctor examined him, he told us that the child's heart was defective and that we should consult with a prominent heart specialist in Vilna.

"The heart specialist said that there was nothing he could do. I cried all night at the inn where we had lodged. One of the other guests asked why I was crying, and when I told her, she said, 'On the way home, stop off in Radin to see the Chofetz Chaim and get a berachah from him.'

"When we reached Radin, we were told that the Chofetz Chaim was old and very weak and that we could not see him. My heart sank, but then I recognized a young man, the Chofetz Chaim's grandson, who had roomed with us when he was at the yeshivah. I pleaded with him, and he arranged for us to see the Chofetz Chaim.

"I bitterly cried out my heart to the Chofetz Chaim, who said, 'Don't cry, my child. Be besimchah [joyous]. Promise me that every Friday you will have the Shabbos table set before noon and the candles ready. Be sure that everything in the kitchen is finished early, and be careful to light the candles well before sunset.' I promised, and he gave us a berachah for a refuah sheleimah [complete recovery].

"I kept my promise to the Chofetz Chaim, and from then on I could see the child developing well. I took him to the doctor, who said, 'Were you at the clinic in Leipzig?' I told him that we had gone to the specialist in Vilna. 'Take him back to Vilna,' he said.

"When the specialist in Vilna saw my son, he said, "This is not the same child you brought here last time.' I told him that he was our only child. He shook his head in amazement. 'There is nothing wrong with the child's heart,' he said. 'I did not want to tell you last time, but your child's heart *was virtually destroyed.' I told him that we had received a berachah from the Chofetz Chaim.*

"The specialist was Jewish but not observant. He said, 'Sometimes there are things we, as doctors, can do for an ailing heart. But to replace a totally defective heart with a new, healthy heart, that is something only the Chofetz Chaim could do.'

"Now you understand," the woman said, "why I am so anxious that my husband return early."

Everyone can implement this wonderful *segulah*. Don't rush into the house two minutes before candle-lighting. Prepare to welcome the Shabbos with joy. Just as the Chofetz Chaim's blessing healed a diseased heart, so it will heal those who are downhearted.

The Midrash says that two angels escort people home from *shul* on Friday evening: a benevolent angel and a malevolent angel. If the house is bright and joyous, the benevolent angel says, "May it be this way next Shabbos," and the malevolent angel must answer, "Amen." If the mood in the house is depressed, the malevolent angel says, "May it be this way next Shabbos," and the benevolent angel is forced to answer, "Amen."

Come into the home with a hearty "Good Shabbos!" Give the children your blessing. Sing *Shalom Aleichem* and *Aishes Chayil*. Reciting the *Hamotzi* (blessing over bread) on the twin challos on Shabbos with the thought that Hashem will provide our food, just as He provided a double portion of manna for our ancestors in the desert, is propitious for a blessing of *parnassah* (livelihood). Sing *zemiros* with lively melodies, and incorporate the meaning of the words: "*Menuchah vesimchah ohr laYehudim* (Contentment and gladness and light for the Jews); *Yom zeh leYisrael orah vesimchah* (This day for Israel is light and gladness) — *Chemdas halevavos l'umah sh'vurah; l'nefashos nechachos neshamah yeseirah, l'nefesh metzeirah tasir anachah* — *Shabbos menuchah* (Heart's beloved of the shattered nation, for suffering people an additional soul, for a troubled soul it removes moaning — Shabbos of contentment)." Repeat this verse both as a praise and as a prayer. Remember that *Mesillas Yesharim* says that one's actions can determine one's mood. You can create *simchah* (gladness).

The prophet says, "For in *simchah* shall you go out" (*Isaiah* 55:12). One of the Chassidic masters said, "With *simchah* one can exit from all *tzaros*."

If you do not have the custom of serving *farfel* (egg barley) Friday night, I suggest that you adopt it. When my mother served the *farfel* she would say, "Whatever was until now is *farfallen* [bygone, over and done with]." *Farfel* is a symbolic reminder to put the past behind us (at least during Shabbos) and look toward the future with hope.

Say a *dvar Torah* at the Shabbos table. Torah words bring

gladness. Listen to what the children have learned during the week. Invite friends for *Kiddush* (refreshments offered in celebration of the Sabbath) on Shabbos morning. Enjoy an afternoon nap.

Sanctify the Shabbos as the Talmud says, "Your speech on Shabbos should be different than the way you speak during the weekdays" (*Shabbos* 113b). Do not read anything pertaining to business on Shabbos. In fact, restrict your reading to Torah literature, There is enough to keep you supplied all day long.

Carry the joy of Shabbos until *Havdalah* (literally separation; the ceremony that ends the Sabbath). I suggest that you preface *Havdalah* with the prayer of R' Levi Yitzchak of Berditchev:

> "G-d of Abraham, of Isaac, and of Jacob, protect Your people, Israel, from all evil. As the holy Shabbos takes leave, may the coming week arrive to bring perfect faith, faith in scholars, love of and attachment to good friends, and attachment to the Creator. May this week arrive for kindness, for good fortune, for blessing, for success, for good health, for wealth and honor, and for children, life, and sustenance for us and for all Israel, Amen."

My father repeated this prayer three times before *Havdalah*.

The *Shulchan Aruch* says that one should be mindful to observe *Melaveh Malkah* (a meal celebrating the departure of the Shabbos Queen). It need not be elaborate. At our home, the menu for *Melaveh Malkah* was simple: herring, borscht, and potatoes. Inspiring stories of *tzaddikim* are related. The *sefarim* say that eating or drinking hot food at *Melaveh Malkah* is conducive to lifting one's spirits.

R' Yehoshua of Kaminka said that relating the following story at *Melaveh Malkah* is a *segulah* for *parnassah*.

(This story may be a synthesis of a midrash and a story about Alexander the Great.)

A man who had fallen on bad times asked the Baal Shem Tov to help him. The Baal Shem Tov told him that if he would dig under a certain bridge, he would find gold. The man did so, but found nothing.

This man happened to get into a conversation with another man who, too, had a tale of woe and said to him, "I asked the Baal Shem Tov for help, and I did what he said, but I found nothing."

"That's strange," the second man said. "I, too, asked the Baal Shem Tov for help, and he told me that I would find a treasure if I dug behind a certain person's house. But I can't go digging up another person's property."

The first man exclaimed, "But that house to which the

Baal Shem Tov directed you is my house!" He rushed home, dug behind his house, and found the treasure. The second man, in the meantime, thought, "Maybe this person did not dig in the right place under the bridge. I'll try my luck." He dug and found the gold.

Each of the two men thought, "How can I enjoy my luck if this other person is impoverished? After all, he was the indirect cause of my finding the wealth. When the two met, ready to share their good fortune with each other, they decided that inasmuch as one of them had a son and the other a daughter, they would make a shidduch between them and give the wealth to their children.

R' Yehoshua of Kaminka said, "There is a treasure that awaits every person, but one cannot get it unless one tries to help others."

A WORD OF ADVICE:

At all times, Shabbos is an oasis of peace in a work-filled week. But in difficult times, Shabbos is also a haven of joy; inculcating the peace and joy of Shabbos will brighten the ensuing weekdays.

8. TEFILLAH

*T*efillah (prayer) is important at all times, but especially when one is in a precarious state.

The word *tefillah* means "bonding" (*Rashi, Genesis* 30:8). When we bond with Hashem, we become more secure.

It is important that *tefillah* be said not only with *kavannah*, but also with *simchah*. R' Nachman of Breslov says, "If a person is not in a joyous mood, he should act as if he were happy, and should sing the *tefillos* (prayers) with a lively melody" (*Likutei Eitzos*). *Sefer Chassidim* (773) says, "When a person *davens* and has the *simchah* of love for Hashem, Hashem will grant his prayers."

We are told that *tefillah* should be with both *yirah* (awe) and *ahavah* (love). At first glance, these seem to be incompatible. Awe is generally not conducive to love. Awe causes one to distance oneself from the awesome object, while love seeks a closer relationship. Nonetheless, in relating to Hashem, the two are fully compatible.

We must understand what is meant by *ahavah* for Hashem. *Ahavah* is generally taken to mean "love"; however, inasmuch as there is a mitzvah of *ahavas Hashem*, the question is asked, "How can a person be commanded to have an emotion?" One can be ordered to *do*, but one cannot be ordered to *feel*.

Rambam dealt with this question, saying, "How does one acquire *ahavah*? If one contemplates Hashem's works and His wondrous creations, and sees in them His infinite wisdom, he will immediately love, praise, and extol Him and have a great desire to know Him" (*Yesodei HaTorah* 2:2).

The commentary on Rambam states that there are two kinds of *ahavah*. One is love, as that of a parent to a child or a husband to a wife, and the second is *admiration*, such that awareness of the greatness of an individual creates a desire to be with that individual. It is the latter type of *ahavah* that the Torah commands man to have for G-d. This kind of admiration-based *ahavah* eventually leads to the *ahavah* that we generally think of as "love."

Essentially, Rambam is giving us a second definition of *ahavah*, which is much different than that which we refer to as "love." This type of *ahavah* is *adoration* rather than love. We may think of it in the way a child feels about a hero, whom he "worships." In some circles, this may often be a sports figure with whom the child is enthralled. He cherishes an autograph of his hero, and would be thrilled if he could own some of his personal memorabilia. If the child were asked to express his most fervent wish, he might well say, "To have dinner with my hero." He does not "love" his hero, but rather has an intense adoration of him.

Adoration of Hashem can indeed be achieved if one has an awareness of His infinite wisdom, which, Rambam says, can be achieved by appreciating the incomparable perfection of His works. Indeed, the more one understands the intricacies of the macrocosm and the microcosm, the more one has *yirah* and stands in awe of Hashem's wisdom. These types of *ahavah* and *yirah* are indeed compatible.

Rambam says that *ahavah* and *yirah* are achieved "if one contemplates Hashem's works and His wondrous creations, and sees in them His infinite wisdom." Unfortunately, we may be derelict in the appreciation of Hashem's great works.

A physician who specializes in infertility problems and who is not a practicing Orthodox Jew said, "I was peering through the microscope at a minuscule fertilized ovum, and I realized that from this point on, all this tiny diploid cell will receive is carbon, oxygen, nitrogen, hydrogen, and a few trace elements, and from those this single cell will be fashioned into a fully functioning human being. At that moment I knew that there is a G-d."

One may not be impacted by this statement unless one understands the marvelous structure of the human body. The liver, which weighs only two kilograms, produces chemical reactions that could not be duplicated by a four-story, fully computerized chemical factory. The kidney, at every moment, decides how much sodium and potassium to keep and how much to excrete; the endocrine system operates with exquisite precision, with delicate checks-and-balances and feedback loops. Yet all these are dwarfed by the central nervous system, comprised of 100 billion cells, all multiply interconnected and operating in a manner that staggers the imagination. At every moment, the cerebellum, from its position beneath the brain, keeps a record of where every single part of the body is at any given time, and brings all these parts into coordination. My neurophysiology professor said, "From the time the pitcher throws the ball until the batter swings at it, hundreds of thousands of messages are communicated through the central nervous system."

Why should a combination of carbon, oxygen, nitrogen, and hydrogen be able to see, hear, and speak? How does the brain, which is a mass of matter, produce thought? How does matter compose the nine symphonies of Beethoven?

To say that the development of a fetus is remarkable is a gross understatement. If the firing off of an enzyme is delayed by a fraction of a second, a congenital abnormality will result. Not even in many trillions of years could evolution produce a human organism. How well did Job put it: "From my flesh I see G-d" (Job 19:26).

Even this awareness is just an infinitesimal fragment of Hashem's greatness. Rambam was right. The more one becomes aware of the marvels of Hashem's creation, the greater are one's *ahavah* and *yirah*, and the more profound is one's *tefillah*. With a better understanding of Hashem's infinite greatness, the greater is the joy of binding oneself to Hashem.

The Chassidic rebbe, R' Yisrael of Husiatin, was hospitalized at an advanced age in Assuta Hospital of Tel Aviv. He asked his doctor for permission to go outdoors, but because it was cold and damp, the doctor would not allow it. After much pleading, the doctor consented; bundled up tightly in scarves and blankets, the rebbe was taken outside for a few moments.

The rebbe looked up at the sky and said, "As long as a person is indoors, one sees the walls and ceiling, constructed by human beings whose thoughts may not have been most noble. When one is outdoors, one sees the world that Hashem created, the earth and the sky that is unchanged since the Six Days of Creation. One is then able to bond with the Creator."

Tefillah can be very inspiring and uplifting, but we must make it so. A father complained that his 11-year-old son did not want to *daven* in spite of being ordered to do so. I told the father that the child had probably not had an opportunity to see *davening* as inspiring. The rushed *davening* at *shul* is, unfortunately, perfunctory. I suggested that every day, for 10 minutes, he learn some small segment of *tefillah* with the child. When the child appreciates the meaning of *tefillah*, he will be more likely to want to *daven*. This is a suggestion for everyone. There are many fine books on *tefillah* that should be studied. When *tefillah* is better understood, it will be more uplifting.

What about when a person feels unable to pray? R' Nachman says:

> When a person finds that he is utterly unable to pray or even to open his mouth because of the severity of his sadness and the bitterness of the darkness, he may perceive himself to be at an unfathomable distance from the Holy One. Even in this hopelessness, he should search and seek within himself a point of merit. He should revive and rejoice through this, because surely every

person is worthy to grow in joy very greatly from each and every good point within himself. When we are in despair, we may look at ourselves and see only unworthiness, but if we search within ourselves for one small point of light that is good and worthy, we will find the one point, and then we must search and find another and another (*Likutei Maharan I*, p. 282).

Everyone can find within himself a point of merit, which can be a fine ray of light, and even a small amount of light can dispel much darkness.

R' Levi Yitzchak of Berditchev, who was renowned for defending every Jew, met a man who was eating on the fast day of Tishah B'Av. He said, "No doubt, my son, you have forgotten that today is Tishah B'Av."

"No," the man said, "I know it is Tishah B'Av."

"Ah!" R' Levi Yitzchak said. "The doctor told you that you should not fast."

"No," the man said, "I am perfectly healthy."

R' Levi Yitzchak exclaimed, "Master of the Universe! See how wonderful Your people are. I gave this man not one, but two opportunities to defend his eating on Tishah B'Av, but he will not budge from the truth!"

We can find merits within ourselves, and we can find points of light in the darkness.

A WORD OF ADVICE:

Davening brings one closer to Hashem. While tefillah should be recited with ahavah and yirah, when one does so with simchah as well, his prayers are more likely to be granted.

9. SIMCHAH SHEL MITZVAH

The Talmud extols the great merit of *simchah shel mitzvah,* the joy that one feels when doing a mitzvah. When one is downhearted, he can lift his spirits by doing a mitzvah.

You might say, "I sure am downhearted. I do the mitzvos, but I cannot say that I am particularly thrilled with them." You are fooling yourself. True, you may now be squeezed financially, but suppose someone came and offered you a huge sum of money to remove all the *mezuzos* from your doorposts or to eat pork. Even if you are desperate for money, you would not do either. Obviously, you value these mitzvos even more than money. And if you just give this some thought, you will realize that you are indeed so happy with these mitzvos that you would not exchange them even for a huge amount of money.

Our concept of *simchah* is too narrow. We generally think of *simchah* as the joyous feeling at a celebration, such as a wedding or *Simchas Torah*. Unfortunately, the idea that *simchah* is limited to feeling happy has contributed to some people trying to attain a happy feeling by using outside stimulants. In *Simchah — It's Not Just Happiness* I pointed out that *simchah* has other meanings as well. For example, *simchah* can refer to the feeling one has upon achieving a level of *sheleimus* (wholeness).

Think of a person who has lost vision or hearing due to an illness, and these are restored during the recovery period. How thrilled the patient is to be able to see and hear again! The loss of these vital functions is depressing, because seeing and hearing are components of a person who is completely healthy.

The human being differs from an animal in that a person has a *spirit*, which I have defined as being comprised of all the uniquely human traits such as being conscious of a goal in life, improving oneself, making moral choices in defiance of bodily urges, and giving of oneself to help strangers. These and other traits are missing in animals and, therefore, define the human being. A person who does not exercise these uniquely human traits is not whole, just as one who is bereft of a vital physical function is lacking wholeness.

In addition to the spirit, we have a *neshamah* (soul) which is of Divine origin. Just as the body and spirit require essential nutrients, without which they are deficient, so, too, the *neshamah* requires its nutrients. The essential nutrients of the *neshamah* are the mitzvos.

In *Happiness and the Human Spirit*, I pointed out that failure to provide the spirit with its nutrients — fulfillment of the uniquely human traits — results in a Spirituality Deficiency Syndrome which is characterized by chronic unhappiness. Similarly, failure to provide the *neshamah* with mitzvos results in a deficiency state that precludes true happiness.

We were created with the mission to do the will of Hashem, and we can be whole only when we achieve this. Doing the mitzvos provides the wholeness without which one cannot have *simchah*. The converse is that when we do mitzvos, we are contributing to *simchah*. Obviously, if one has suffered adversity, one may be in pain, just as when one has sustained a physical injury, but even in adversity one can have the *simchah* of feeling whole.

R' Samson Raphael Hirsch says that the Hebrew words *same'ach* (happy) and *tzome'ach* (growth) are almost identical, because *simchah* is the outcome of spiritual growth. Thus, the growth achieved by fulfilling the mission for which we were created leads to *simchah*.

Those people who think that *simchah* occurs only in joyous celebration, much like the sugar high obtained from eating sweets or imbibing soft drinks, are shortsighted. While this kind of joy is indeed commendable, it is nevertheless of a fleeting nature. The *simchah* of doing mitzvos is enduring. The wholeness achieved by doing mitzvos does not dissipate soon thereafter.

You observe the mitzvos because you believe in Hashem. Suppose you received a call from the president of the United States, asking you to do something. How thrilled and honored you would be. "Imagine! The president himself called me!" Inasmuch as you believe in Hashem and do the mitzvos that He commanded, it is a far greater honor to be asked to do something by the King of the universe than by a mortal head of state. Again, if you think about it, you will feel the joy of doing a mitzvah.

Every mitzvah that you do creates an angel that will be your advocate. If you got a traffic ticket and received a call from the mayor saying, "Don't worry about it. I'll see that it is taken care of," wouldn't you feel thrilled that the mayor agreed to advocate for you? How much more thrilling that you now have angels, created by your mitzvos, that will advocate for you!

The psalmist says, "Light is sown for the righteous; and for the upright of heart, gladness. Be glad, O righteous, in Hashem ..." (*Psalms* 97:11-12).

A WORD OF ADVICE:

The simchah of doing a mitzvah lifts one out of the doldrums and elevates one's spirits.

10. Living With a Purpose

Sometimes it takes a crisis to set us to thinking about what our lives are all about — or rather, what our lives *should be* all about.

I once made a *shivah* call (condolence visit) to a family that had lost a child. As I left the home with a friend, he said, "King Solomon said, 'It is better to go to a house of mourning than to go to a house of feasting, for that is the end of all man, and the living should take it to heart' [*Ecclesiastes* 7:2]. I never quite understood what it is that we are to take to heart. But when I heard the bereaved parents say, 'Why did she die?' I could not help but think that we rarely, if ever, ask the question, 'Why are we alive?'"

It is true. When our lives flow along smoothly, we generally do not give much thought to why we are alive, and what the purpose of our lives is. However, although we may not think about this consciously, the question may gnaw away at us in our unconscious mind, which is the repository of those thoughts we would rather not think about.

The reason that this thought is not well tolerated in the conscious mind is because we do not have a strong concept of an ultimate purpose. We know the purpose of many things we do. The purpose of pulling up at the gas pump is to buy fuel so that we can drive to the office, and the purpose of our going to the office is to do whatever it is we do there. We have a series of *intermediate* purposes, but we rarely reflect on an ultimate purpose.

My father told the story of a man who was sentenced to 25 years of hard labor. His hands were shackled to the handle of a massive wheel set in the wall, and during his waking hours he had to turn the massive wheel. He would often wonder what he was accomplishing. Perhaps he was grinding grain, or providing water for irrigation. At the end of the 25 years he was released, and the first thing he did was to rush to the other side of the wall. He was shocked to see that the wheel was not attached to anything, and he collapsed. Twenty-five years of backbreaking labor — all for nothing! He had survived those 25 years of torture, but could not survive the awareness that his work had been without purpose.

But of course we have a purpose. We provide for the family, we contribute to the community and we give a helping hand to the needy. Aren't those noble purposes?

Of course they are, but I am reminded of the two loiterers who were arrested for vagrancy and brought before the judge. The judge addressed the first vagrant, "What were you doing when the officer arrested you?"

The vagrant replied, "I wasn't doing anything."

The judge then turned to the second vagrant, "And what were you doing when you were arrested?"

The second vagrant pointed to his buddy, "I was helping him," he said.

Our purpose may be doing things for people, but unless *those* people have a purpose, we are similar to the vagrant who was helping his buddy do nothing.

But all of us do have a purpose, and that is to serve Hashem. If that is what gives meaning to our lives, then it should be of the greatest importance. A chassid was asked, "What is most important to your Rebbe?" and he answered, "Whatever he happens to be doing at the time, because if there were anything more important, he would be doing that." If we are not engaged in serving Hashem, it is because we do not see that as the most important thing in our lives.

The *sefarim* say that serving Hashem is not limited to the performance of the mitzvos. If we eat in order to have the energy to do the mitzvos, if we sleep so that we can be alert to do the mitzvos, and if we work or engage in business in order to have the means to do the mitzvos, then those activities of daily life that enable us to do the mitzvos are all in the service of Hashem. But in order to qualify as service of Hashem, we must consciously dedicate all our activities to the service of Hashem. They do not take on that quality automatically.

Eventually, the economy will recover and our lives will stabilize. It is then that we must remember to continue to give true meaning to our lives, not to wait for another crisis to motivate us to do so.

A WORD OF ADVICE:

When we conduct our lives with the purpose of serving Hashem, we give true meaning to all our endeavors.

11. Don't Open Yourself Up to Risk!

You have always been able to provide your family with a pleasant lifestyle. Suddenly you find yourself in a financial squeeze. You don't want to disappoint your family, so you may try to get money in any possible way. You are so driven by this that your judgment may be seriously impaired, and you may be oblivious to the consequences of your actions.

You might decide to gamble at the racetrack, hope to hit the jackpot at a casino, or try your luck at cards. You say, "I won't be reckless. I'll try for a win, and then I'll quit." You are deceiving yourself. You can get carried away by the urge to amass a great deal of money quickly. You may say, "I'm different. I won't lose control." In any addictive behavior, the two words, "I'm different," are fatal. Similarly, do not borrow money from loan sharks.

I received the following inquiry from a desperate woman.

My husband always made a nice parnassah and was able to support the family in a comfortable way and give tzeddakah. He never shared his business dealings with me. Lately he is very nervous and uptight. He does not sleep well at night. He told me that we would have to cut our spending drastically. Recently he's been having meetings in the dining room behind closed doors. I don't like the looks of the people he's meeting with, nor do I like the tone of voice I hear through the doors. After doing some investigation on my own, I found out that my husband had borrowed money on the "gray market." I fear for his life. What should I do?

I responded:

If you suspect that your husband is getting money in a risky way, whether by borrowing from the mob, gambling, or in any other way that can be dangerous, he must be confronted. If you try to confront him yourself, he will most likely just brush you off. Reasoning with him is likely to be futile. He must be saved from himself. Furthermore, this kind of action can bring disaster to the whole family.

This requires a confrontation (which in the addiction field is called an "intervention"), and requires assembling a number of people who have his interest at heart (yourself, parents, parents-in-law, rabbi, close friends) and rehearsing with an "intervention specialist." The intervention specialist will coach the participants with regard to how to confront the addict. He or she will provide guidance both on what must be said and, even more important, on what must not be said. The group, as a unit, then meets with him and makes it clear that he must discontinue the potentially destructive behavior. If treatment is necessary, the specialist can arrange for that. You can reach an intervention specialist by contacting an alcohol/drug treatment program. Although he is not an addict, the intervention process is the same.

When someone is desperate for money, especially to support the family or to meet commitments, one may turn to gambling in the hope of striking it rich. The worst thing that can happen is that one may make an initial win. If a person has an innate propensity toward compulsive gambling, this can be the beginning of an addiction that can prove disastrous to the whole family. The wife's jewelry may be sold, and the house may be mortgaged and the mortgage payment not met, without the wife's knowledge.

A spouse may not want to tell his/her parents, in-laws, or rabbi. This is a mistake. Compulsive gambling is a cancerous behavior that may require drastic measures.

The problem of compulsive gambling is not uncommon in the Jewish community. The family may close its eyes to the problem, or what is worse, will bail out the gambler from his debts. They may fear that if the problem is exposed, it may affect the family reputation or cause a *chilul Hashem* (desecration of G-d's Name). While these concerns are certainly understandable, the fact is that in every case I know of where there has been a cover-up, the gambling progressed to the point that the exposure was of even greater magnitude of humiliation and expense.

If the gambler violates the law, by credit card fraud, forged checks, or stealing (even if it's from the family), the family may hire a lawyer to extract the gambler from his legal problems. They may accept his promises that he will never do it again. *This is a mistake!* He is making a promise that he cannot keep. He may be making a promise in good faith, truly believing that he will fulfill his vow, but he cannot. The only thing that can bring a compulsive gambler to his senses is experiencing the consequences of his gambling. If the family "rescues" him, they are eliminating the sole impetus that can motivate him to seek help. If one suspects that a family member may be gambling, one should promptly consult an expert on the problem for guidance.

At the risk of being accused of commercializing, I suggest

that we all familiarize ourselves with problem gambling by reading *Compulsive Gambling — More Than Dreidle*. It's better to be forewarned than sorry.

A WORD OF ADVICE:

Assuming numerous loans at exorbitant interest rates or resorting to gambling to pay your debts is a surefire road to addictive behavior. Do not allow yourself to be lured into this trap!

12. DEALING WITH THE STRESS

Although much has been written about coping with stress, it is important to understand stress and how to deal with it.

An enthusiastic young salesman tried to sell a farmer an almanac. "This book tells you when to plow, when to sow, when to water, and when to reap," the young man said.

The farmer responded, "Young feller, I know all that already. Problem is getting to do it."

In much the same way, perhaps reviewing what we know can help us to implement a plan of action.

Some people have never experienced stress of this magnitude. It is important that we understand the nature of stress and what accommodations we can make.

Let me explain the "fight or flight" response, which occurs with severe stress.

Human beings are endowed with adaptive capacities for coping. The adaptive features comprise the "fight or flight" reaction, which is designed to enable escape from an assailant or to facilitate defensive action. A number of physiologic changes occur upon the perception of a threat. Understanding these may help us better understand and cope with anxiety.

When threatened with danger, the heart rate increases sharply in order to supply oxygen-carrying blood to the muscles. Respiration increases to inhale more oxygen and dispose of carbon dioxide. The blood supply shifts from the digestive tract to the muscles where it is most likely to be needed. The blood is diverted from the body surface to minimize blood loss from wounds. (This is the reason for pallor.) The liver discharges its storage of glucose to provide nutrients for the muscles. The coagulation time of the blood decreases to minimize hemorrhage. The pupils of the eyes dilate. The blood pressure rises as adrenaline and cortisonelike hormones are secreted into the blood stream.

These physiologic changes are very effective in adaptation to an acute assault, whether by animal or man. They enhance the body's ability to run away or to defend itself. In most cases, the confrontation between the attacker and victim is of brief duration. Within a few brief moments, one of the following will have occurred: One has either managed to flee, has subdued the assailant, or has been killed.

The human psyche perceives a variety of threats as an acute attack. A serious threat to one's financial well-being or an assault on one's ego is regarded as an attack, and the body may trigger the physiologic changes of the fight-or-flight reaction. *However, in this case, they are not effective.* That is because there is no safe haven to which one can escape and there is nothing one can do to fight off a non-corporal assailant. Furthermore, in contrast to an acute attack, the anxiety is not over within a few moments. To the contrary, it may persist throughout the day and night, for weeks and months. These persistent body changes, which in these circumstances are not adaptive, may exert great stress on the body and they may result in physical as well as psychological disorders.

In addition to cardiovascular effects, diabetes may develop, the immune system may be suppressed, the inflammatory response may be inhibited, there may be an increase in abdominal fat, acceleration of the aging process, impairment of memory and learning, and, in children, inhibition of growth. (Make no mistake. Children feel the stress of the economic crisis.)

It is, therefore, vital that one finds ways to reduce the stress.

I know what you are thinking. "Get me a job. Enable me to support my family the way I was accustomed to, and I won't have the stress." How I wish I could do so! But we cannot live with wishful thinking. Reality is what it is.

"So, now you are going to tell me I should do breathing exercises and progressive muscle relaxation? You want me to meditate in my condition?"

You are already meditating. When you brood over the losses you have experienced, you are, in fact, meditating. But inasmuch as brooding will not improve your situation one iota, you are engaging in negative meditation. Since you are already meditating, why not switch to positive meditation? It can be done.

There may be a number of things you can do to adapt to your present situation, but like Hagar in the desert, your stress level may not enable you to see and utilize them. Meditation has been proven to be effective even in situations of severe stress. You have probably been brooding much more than 20 minutes a day. You should invest 20 minutes in meditation.

But isn't meditation associated with eastern religions? No way! There is much in Torah literature on meditation. The Talmud states, "The pious of yore would meditate an hour before prayer and an hour after prayer" (*Berachos* 30b). Chassidic writings stress the importance of *hisboddedus* (seclusion) and *hisbonnenus* (meditation). Chassidic masters were known to go off into the woods and meditate for hours at a time.

Avail yourself of the book, *Jewish Meditation — A Practical Guide*, by Rabbi Aryeh Kaplan. Applying its advice can be extremely helpful in relieving your stress.

You might say, "I can't sit still to meditate. I feel I am sitting on *shpilkes* [pins]." If there is something constructive that you can do to better your situation, by all means do it. But if there is nothing you can do at the moment, why can't you sit still for 15 minutes?

I'll tell you why, from my personal experience.

After an extended period of constant stress, day and night, as director of a large psychiatric hospital and emergency service, I felt I needed a vacation of absolute rest. No activities, not even pleasurable activities. Just rest.

I went to Hot Springs, Arkansas for a vacation, hoping that the mineral baths would relieve my chronic back pain. I was ushered into a tiny room and immersed in a whirlpool bath of naturally heated water. This was just the peace I needed. I could not be reached by patients, families, doctors, nurses, social workers, or probation officers. After five minutes of paradise I emerged and said to the attendant, "This was great! Just what I needed!" The attended told me that I must stay in the whirlpool bath for an additional 20 minutes, or I would not be able to continue with the treatment.

After five more minutes I felt I had to get out of the bath. Later that day I realized that I had had a rude awakening. I was able to tolerate months of constant pressure, but was unable to tolerate more than five minutes of blissful peace! Something was wrong.

A psychologist friend told me that few people know how to relax. Most people engage in some diversion in order to relax, such as reading a book, listening to music, playing golf, or doing needlework. But true relaxation is an absence of any kind of action. Diversions are fine, but they are not relaxation.

In the whirlpool cubicle, I was deprived of all diversions. Nothing to read, nothing to listen to, nothing to do. With nothing to distract me, I was left in immediate contact with *myself*, and I did not like the company I was in!

If one cannot sit still for 15 minutes to meditate, it is probably because he does not want to be in contact with himself. Developing healthy self-esteem will enable one to sit still long enough to meditate. Work at improving your self-esteem. *Ten Steps to Being Your Best* can help you make a good beginning.

The Talmud interprets, "When there is worry in a man's heart, he should suppress it [by sharing it with others], let a good thing convert it to gladness" (*Proverbs* 12:25), to mean that when one has a worry, one should discuss it with someone else (*Yoma* 25a). This is one of the foundations of psychotherapy. However, this does not necessarily mean that you should discuss your problems with a therapist. It may be helpful to share your worries with a friend.

> *A man who had lost his entire family in the Holocaust came to see the tzaddik, R' Ahron of Belz. He bitterly poured out his heart to the tzaddik and said, "Who else could understand my pain like the Rebbe, who also experienced such a bad fate and lost his whole family?"*
>
> *The Rebbe arose and in a voice of intense emotion said, "Chas veshalom [Heaven forbid]! Hashem has never done anything bad to me! Hashem has only done good to me!" He told the man to leave the room and wash his hands, and when the man returned, the Rebbe said, "Retract your words! Hashem does only good!"*

We may not be able to achieve the level of *emunah* (faith) of the *tzaddik*, but ventilating your worries with a friend may help you see some things you may have overlooked. It is not unusual that in describing a problem to a therapist, one discovers a solution.

R' Elimelech of Lizhensk suggests an additional reason for the effectiveness of sharing a worry. "Assume," he says, "that for reasons known only to Hashem, it was decreed that Reuven experience a degree of suffering. Reuven then unburdens himself to his friend, Shimon, who is distressed by his friend Reuven's suffering. Inasmuch as it was never decreed that Shimon should suffer, Shimon's distress does not meet the criteria of Hashem's justice. Therefore, to relieve Shimon of his unwarranted distress, Hashem will relieve Reuven of his suffering."

You may know of a friend who lost his job, and he may be hesitant to talk about it. You should initiate the contact. Visit him and allow him to vent. There might not be anything tangible that you can do for him, yet if you feel for him and sincerely say, "If there is any way I can be of help, please call me," that is comforting.

The Baal Shem Tov commented on the verse, "Hashem is your shadow" (*Psalms* 121:5), "Just as a person's shadow mimics every move one makes, so does Hashem relate to a person according to one's actions. If you help others, Hashem will help you."

We cannot know when we may need help. I remember as a child reading the fable of a lion who caught a mouse. The mouse pleaded, "Let me go. One day I will save you." The lion released the mouse and roared with laughter. The king of the jungle is going to be saved by a tiny mouse!

One day the lion was trapped by a hunter's net. The mouse came and said, "Don't worry. I will gnaw through the ropes and I will set you free." Yes, the tiny mouse saved the king of the jungle.

In lieu of ventilating to someone, it is helpful to keep a journal, writing down the problems. Of what value is this? It may help you get them off your mind, where you have been ruminating about what has happened. Seeing the problem set down in writing may help you better control a difficult situation. Do not minimize the effectiveness of writing. On Rosh Hashanah we are not satisfied with praying, "Remember us for life," but we also pray, "*Inscribe us* in the book of life, of *parnassah*, of forgiveness, of salvation," even though Hashem's memory is perfect and He has no need to record His decisions. There is a special effectiveness when something is written, and the act of recording your problems may help you discover solutions.

Speaking about journalizing, begin a "gratitude journal." You may be so preoccupied with your problems that you lose sight of the things for which you should be grateful. Too often, we take things for granted. *Baruch Hashem* (thank G-d), your children are healthy. You thank Hashem every morning that you are alive, and say *berachos* (blessings) of gratitude for being able to arise and to walk. Very often, we say these *berachos* without giving them due thought. It is a *chesed* (act of grace) that we can walk and talk. Sometimes we are reminded of this only when we see someone who has lost these abilities. Keeping a gratitude journal encourages positive thinking.

And, if you think that some of your problems were brought on by mistakes you made, such as unwise investments, make a section of the journal for "Dumb things I did," and record your mistakes. That way, you don't have to keep thinking about them. You can always find them in your journal if you need to.

> *My father had two landsleit (fellow countrymen), Moshe and Chaim, who met on one occasion when they visited him. Moshe had come to America as a young man, and was very enterprising. He started a storefront laundry, and eventually developed a very profitable laundry and a linen-supply business. Chaim, on the other hand, had a corner grocery and barely eked out a living. Although Moshe was quite wealthy, he was miserable. He suffered from stomach ulcers, and in those days there was really no treatment for that condition. Moshe lived on soda crackers and milk.*
>
> *When they met, Moshe asked Chaim, "Nu, how are things with you?" Chaim sighed and said, "Not good, Moshe. I have to be up at 4 o'clock in the morning to go to the market. Then I have to stand on my feet all day until 9 o'clock at night. And what do I earn from all this? All I can afford to eat is dark bread and radish."*
>
> *Moshe said, "Chaim, you are a fool! I would gladly give away both my businesses to be able to eat dark bread and radish!"*

In spite of your hardships, you have much for which you can be grateful.

It is related that a man whose house burned down recited the berachah, "shelo asani goy." He explained that if he had been an idol worshiper, his god would have been destroyed along with his house. However, although he lost his house, he still has his G-d.

As part of a study done in a major psychiatric center, depressed patients were made to exercise daily; they were compared to patients who took antidepressant medication. The therapeutic results were equal. Apparently exercise stimulates production of adrenalinelike substances that can alleviate depression. You may say that you are not in the mood to exercise. That is understandable, but exercise is one way of decreasing the severity of the depressive mood.

A friend told me that when he heard and saw the attack on the World Trade Center, he went out and did some gardening. He was not callous. He said, "I felt I had to do something over which I had some control."

Obviously, we have no control over the economy, and it is a terrible feeling, much like being caught in a tornado. We may regain a bit of composure by doing something we *can* control.

In addition to doing something one can control, there is benefit in doing something, *anything*. I do not mean that one should just occupy himself at random and not try to do whatever he can to improve his situation. Rather, when one cannot see anything he can do to better his situation, ruminating about how bad things are achieves nothing, and may blind one to opportunities that might arise. One way to avoid negative rumination is to take action, whether it is to clean out the garage or to paint a room that needs painting. It sounds silly? So let it sound silly. It is still better than actively thinking negative thoughts that cannot be of any use. Two conflicting thoughts cannot occupy the mind at the same time. If one broods on the negative, positive thoughts are blocked out.

If a friend has invited you to a wedding, by all means go and dance. You may not feel like dancing, but *Mesillas Yesharim (Path of the Just)* says that one's actions can determine one's mood. It is amazing what a little bit of *simchah* can do. This was actually stated by the author of *Sefer HaChinuch* (Mitzvah 16). Six hundred years later, the American psychologist William James said, "Action seems to follow feeling, but really action and feeling go together; and by regulating the action, which is under the more direct control of the will, we can indirectly regulate the feeling, which is not. Thus, the sovereign voluntary path to cheerfulness, if your cheerfulness be lost, is to sit up cheerfully and to act and speak as if cheerfulness were already there" (cited in *How to Stop Worrying and Start Living*, pp. 122-123).

Look for opportunities to help someone in any way. That is a good feeling, and good feelings eradicate bad feelings.

The economic crisis is one that touches the entire community, not only in curtailing charitable support but also in causing depression throughout the community. Not everyone knows just who has been affected, and because some people are embarrassed by their severe financial loss, they may withdraw socially. Rabbis should address the problem from the pulpit and provide words of hope and *chizuk.*

There are some affluent people who, even if they have sustained a loss, are still quite wealthy. When they marry off a son or daughter, they may make a lavish wedding. I am sure that we have all attended weddings where the money spent on the trimmings could support a needy family for a year. True, the wealthy have a right to do whatever they wish with their money, but I suggest that at this point we should be very sensitive to the feelings of those whose losses prevent them from making a lavish wedding, and who may be distressed that they cannot provide the kind of wedding they would like for their child.

R' Avigdor Miller explained why an *ayin hara* (evil eye) can cause harm. If a person flaunts his good fortune, it may cause those who are less fortunate to be distressed, and if a person causes others to suffer, he may be taken to task for it. Especially in hard times, it is imperative to be extra sensitive to other people's feelings.

The Torah relates that when the severe famine struck the

Mideast in Joseph's time, Jacob said to his sons, "Why do you make yourselves conspicuous?" (*Genesis* 42:1). Rashi explained that at that time, Jacob's family still had food, and Jacob was saying, "If you don't go to Egypt for food like the others, you will be flaunting what you have and you will elicit the envy of our neighbors." The Torah teaches us not to flaunt our good fortune.

Do say *Tehillim* (*Psalms*) — and read the translation. King David says, "My soul is utterly confounded, and You, Hashem, how long? … I am wearied with my sigh, every night I drench my bed, with tears I soak my couch" (*Psalms* 6:4,7).

"How long, Hashem, will You endlessly forget me? … How long must I set schemes within myself, is my heart melancholy even by day?" (ibid. 13:2,3).

"For my loins are full of a loathsome affliction and there is no soundness in my flesh. I am faint and crushed exceedingly" (ibid. 38:8-9).

Yet, this same King David rises above his distress. "But You have put gladness in my heart" (ibid. 4:8).

"My soul will exult in Hashem, rejoice in His salvation" (ibid. 35:9).

When we are in agony, we can identify with King David's suffering, but we can also be comforted by his unrelenting hope for salvation.

Laughter reduces stress. You may say, "What should I laugh about? My *tzaros*?" I know you are in distress. Nevertheless, find something that you can laugh about. I read that one of the *gedolim* (Torah giants) saw a man who was drowning. He did not know how to swim, but he was able to throw him a rope. He shouted, "Catch hold of the rope, or else give my regards to the Leviathan." He said that he made the wisecrack to try to diminish the man's anxiety so that he would take hold of the rope.

It has been demonstrated that people with serious illnesses, even cancer, have better outcomes of healing and recovery if they can laugh. I had a friend who had cancer. We decided that, every day, I would fax him a joke and he would fax me one. His wife told me that this helped pull him out of depression.

At a psychiatric convention, I saw the psychiatrist near me place his hand at the corners of his mouth and raise them as if he were smiling. He said, "This is not a mannerism. I believe that smiling is very healthy. I don't have anything in particular to smile about today, so I manufacture a smile."

———

I heard a parable that I did not appreciate initially, but as I thought about it, it did make sense.

A man was being chased by a tiger. With nowhere to go, he jumped off a cliff, where he hung on to a vine. Then the man noticed a hungry tiger waiting for him down below. So what did he do? He plucked a grape from the vine and ate it, enjoying its sweetness.

How can one enjoy the sweetness of a grape when suspended between two tigers? Not eating the grape is not going to make his situation less precarious, so why not enjoy what he can? As depressed as one may be with his situation, will denying himself the enjoyment he can have make the situation any better?

———

Severe losses may result in *denial*, whereby a person avoids dealing with a problem as if it did not exist. For example, I received this query.

We live in Lakewood. My parents have supported us for many years. We have eight children; the oldest just had his bar mitzvah. A few years ago my father bought us a house. The mortgage was paid directly from his office. This week I received a call from the bank to inform us that the mortgage had not been paid for the past three months. They threatened us with foreclosure. I am embarrassed to approach my father. What should I do?

I understand and empathize with this woman's distress. She knows that telling her father about the unpaid mortgage and the threat of foreclosure will be painful to him, and she does not want to hurt him. But does she really have a choice? If the house is lost by foreclosure, the pain will be much greater. The fact that the father did not tell the children, "I was hit hard and I will not be able to continue paying the mortgage. Let's see how we can manage," indicates that he was in denial and tried to avoid the unpleasant news.

Denial of a problem does not relieve stress. It merely delays dealing with the situation, which invariably escalates the longer one postpones acknowledging the problem.

Remember, stress begets stress and negative thinking begets negative thinking. Anything you can do to minimize the effects of the stress will put you into a better position to cope with your challenges.

A WORD OF ADVICE:

One's actions determine one's mood. Brooding on the negative leaves no room for positive thoughts. Make a list of all your problems. Then list all the things for which you should be grateful. You may be surprised to see that the positives surely exceed the negatives!

13. HAVE WE BEEN LISTENING TO OUR *DAVENING*?

Generally, when a person is hurt, it is not the time to give *mussar*. If someone slips on the ice and is injured, it is simply cruel to say, "You should be careful when you walk on the ice." The person knows very well that one must exercise care when the sidewalk is icy. Helping the person rise and saying, "I'm sorry you were hurt," is much more appropriate. Reprimanding one for not being careful is unkind.

The person who slipped on the ice knows what happened and why, and he will generally be more careful without your telling him. However, there is an exception to the rule of not giving *mussar*. In the past 40 years of treating alcoholic persons, I have found that when the alcoholic experiences negative effects of his drinking, he is generally oblivious to them. The intensity of the denial in the alcoholic is such that if one does not see it, one would not believe it.

The alcoholic totals his car by wrapping it around a tree, and he has no inkling that his drinking had anything to do with it. He is given many warnings and many "last chances" at work, and when the boss' patience runs out and he is fired, he believes that the boss is picking on him unfairly. After numerous pleadings, his wife leaves him, and he does not have the slightest idea why. That is why Alcoholics Anonymous refers to alcoholism as "insanity." They say that repeating the same act and expecting different results is insanity. The alcoholic needs to be repeatedly told that his troubles are due to his drinking. After many such episodes, it may finally sink in.

There seems to be this kind of denial in the financial world as well. We simply do not seem to realize the unreliability of the "unsinkable" companies.

Years ago, it was quipped that someone in Chicago called railroad information and asked, "When is the last train to New

York?" and was told, "You should live so long," meaning that there would *always* be another train. That did not turn out to be so great a blessing. The mighty Pennsylvania Railroad has disappeared off the map. I recall when Pan Am and TWA airlines were thought to be invincible. The list of multibillion-dollar firms, such as Enron and Bear Sterns, that no longer exist has expanded by leaps and bounds. Just a few years ago, one would have been thought insane had he predicted that mighty General Motors would become bankrupt.

Every morning we say, "Do not rely on nobles, nor on a human being, for he holds no salvation. When his spirit departs, he returns to his earth, on that day his plans all perish"(*Psalms* 146:3-4). The "nobles" are the multibillion-dollar conglomerates.

Moses warned the Israelites, "… everything that you have will increase …. And you may say in your heart, 'My strength and the might of my hand made me all this wealth!' Then you shall remember Hashem, your G-d: that it was He Who gave you strength to make wealth …" (*Deuteronomy* 8:13-18). It is noteworthy that Targum Onkeles translates the latter part of the verse, "It was He Who gave you the judgment to acquire possessions." These verses do not mean that one should not engage in commerce and make investments. The Torah says, "Hashem will bless you in all your handwork *that you do*" (emphasis added) (*Deuteronomy* 14:29). Obviously, we must do. Rather, the Torah means that we should not let our ego become too arrogant. If we think we can control our destiny, we will find out differently.

A person should do proper research when making an investment, and then pray to Hashem for guidance and success. Ultimately, the will of Hashem will prevail.

A man carrying a heavy suitcase was walking along the side of the road, when a wagon passed by and the driver offered the man a ride. The man gratefully accepted and climbed aboard. After a bit, the driver noticed that the man was still holding his suitcase.

"Why don't you set the bag down?" he asked.

The man replied, "I'm very thankful to you that you are giving me a ride. You don't have to shlep my suitcase, too."

How foolish! We don't make Hashem's task easier by making extra exertions! He carries us effortlessly, no matter how heavy our burdens.

It is noteworthy that in the Shabbos *Nishmas* prayer, after recounting how Hashem saved us from many perils, we say, "… in plenty You provided for us." When the economy was thriving and we were doing well, we might not have realized that Hashem was providing for us. We need to remember that our own unaided efforts would have achieved nothing, and that whatever success we had was a *berachah* from Hashem.

A WORD OF ADVICE:

Paying attention to the words of our prayers will reinforce the knowledge that Hashem is in charge of the world and that everything He does is good.

14. The Mystery of *Yissurim*

O ur nation came into being with *yissurim* (suffering), after decades of inhumane and dehumanizing enslavement in Egypt. Moses referred to this agonizing experience as an "iron crucible" (*Deuteronomy* 4:20), which, Rashi explains "is used to purify gold and purge it of foreign elements." Why did we need to be purged, and why in so harsh a manner?

Our history has been a litany of suffering: exile, expulsion, auto-da-fé, pogroms, Holocaust. But Hashem is the absolute good, compassionate, merciful, gracious, abundant in kindness.

He is our Father, Whose love for us far surpasses that of a human father. How are we to reconcile this with our history of suffering?

Our great teacher, Moses, had the boldness to challenge Hashem. "Why have You done evil to this people? ... From the time I came to Pharaoh to speak in Your Name he did evil to this people, but You did not rescue Your people" (*Exodus* 5:22-23) After the deliverance from Egypt, Moses asked Hashem, "Make Your way known to me" (ibid. 33:13). The Talmud says that Moses asked for an explanation of suffering, but Hashem told him that it could not be understood by anyone who inhabits a physical body (*Berachos* 7a). Only after life is over will this be revealed to us. Indeed, the Talmud says that Moses wrote the *Book of Job*, wherein various explanations for suffering are presented, but all are rebutted (*Bava Basra* 14b). In *Ethics of the Fathers* 4:19, R' Yannai says, "It is not in our power to explain either the tranquility of the wicked or the suffering of the righteous." Suffering, both that of the nation and that of the individual, remains an unfathomable mystery.

It is related that during the lifetime of the Baal Shem Tov's successor, R' DovBer, the Maggid of Mezeritch, there were no anti-Semitic decrees, but they were reinstated after his demise. One of his disciples wondered, "Inasmuch as the Talmud says, 'Tzaddikim are greater after their death than in their lifetime' [Chullin 7b], why was the Maggid able to annul harsh decrees during his lifetime, but does not do so now?"

The Maggid appeared to him in a dream and said, "When I was alive, and with my human eyes I saw that a decree was evil, I intervened to annul it. However, now I can see the ultimate good that will come from these decrees, and I cannot annul something that is for the good."

We believe, we have faith, but we cannot understand. From a logical point of view, suffering remains a mystery.

There are conflicting attitudes in the Talmud toward suffering. The Sage, R' Elazar ben R' Shimon, welcomed suffering, and referred to his agonies as "my brothers, my friends" (*Bava Metzia* 84b). On the other hand, some of the Sages said, "I do not want the agonies nor do I want their reward."

Tzaddikim who welcomed suffering said that a man who had been sinful stood before the Heavenly Tribunal, which was about to pass a harsh sentence on him. A benevolent angel presented the Tribunal with all the sufferings the man had undergone, and the Tribunal reduced the severity of his sentence, whereupon the man said, "If only I had suffered more, all my sins would have been erased."

> There is a parable about a wealthy man who found that money had been stolen from him. He accused one of his servants and took the servant to court. Although the servant denied that he had taken the money, the judge found him guilty and sentenced him to 20 lashes. Some time later, the actual thief was apprehended, and the judge ruled that the master must compensate the innocent servant for having been punished unjustly. The judge ruled that for each lash, the master must give him a gold piece. The servant complained to the judge, "Why did you sentence me to only 20 lashes? If I had received more lashes, I would receive more gold."

My father explained that when the Tetragrammeton, the commonly used four-letter Name of Hashem, is used, it refers to His conducting the world with *chesed*, and when the Name *Elokim* is used, it refers to His conducting the world with stern judgment. We must believe that everything Hashem does is actually *chesed*, although to us some things may appear to be very harsh judgments. What we see may conflict with what we believe. We must conclude that in truth all is really *chesed*, and we cannot rely on what we perceive with our vision. When we say the *Shema*, we assert that both types of conduct — that which we see as *chesed* (represented by the Tetragrammeton) and that which we see as harsh judgment (represented by *Elokim*) are one and the same (Hashem *Echad* — Hashem is One). Inasmuch as our human vision refutes this, we cover our eyes when we say the first verse of the *Shema*, to indicate that we negate what we see with our eyes in favor of what we believe; namely, that all that Hashem does is *chesed*, even if we cannot see it as such.

We are more likely to side with the Sages who said, "I do not want the agonies and I do not want their reward." This is certainly understandable, but we should also try to understand those *tzaddikim* who welcomed suffering.

Perhaps we cannot comprehend someone like R' Zushe of Anipole, who was always in good cheer in spite of being destitute and suffering from physical ailments.

> A man asked R' Zushe's rebbe, the Maggid of Mezeritch, how the Talmud can require a person to praise Hashem for the adversities one suffers. The Maggid directed him to R' Zushe.
>
> R' Zushe concealed his scholarship, and said, "You must be mistaken. I know nothing of the Talmud. I can't answer your question."
>
> "No," the man said, "the Rebbe said to ask the man sweeping the floor. How can the Talmud require a person to praise Hashem for the adversities one suffers?"
>
> R' Zushe said, "I told you, I can't answer your question. You see, I've never suffered any adversity, so how would I know?"

The man had his answer.

———•◦•———

A person asked R' Zushe, "How can you make the berachah, 'Blessed are You, Hashem, Who has provided me with every need,' when you lack the basic necessities of life?"

R' Zushe answered, "Hashem knows what my needs are better than I do, and He knows that one of my needs is poverty."

Tzaddikim who experienced yissurim never lost their trust in Hashem. They knew that Hashem is a loving Father, and as such, whatever He does to His children is out of love for them. Granted, with our limited wisdom, we may have some difficulty understanding this.

Perhaps this anecdote might help us to grasp this concept. I was at a pediatrician's office; a jolly infant there was playing and smiling. When the white-clad doctor came into the room, the baby emitted a shriek and clung to his mother. From previous experiences, the infant knew what was coming: this white-clad monster stabs little children and makes them hurt for two days! To the infant's astonishment, the mother took him into the torture chamber. The infant kicked and fought the mother, who had suddenly become the enemy and was collaborating with the monster. The mother restrained the infant while the doctor administered the injection.

When the doctor left, the infant threw his arms around his mother's neck and held on for dear life. I wondered, Why is the infant clinging to his mother for protection and comfort? Isn't she the one who allowed him to be stabbed? How can she be trusted?

The answer is that although the infant cannot possibly understand that the painful injection is necessary in order to protect him from dreaded diseases, and he cannot fathom why the mother would participate in his being hurt, the child does know that the mother is the person who loves him the most and would give her life to protect him. This aberration — the mother's collaboration with the monster — does not diminish the child's trust in his mother.

We must understand that Hashem's love for us is boundless. The gap between our minds and the infinite wisdom of Hashem is greater than the gap between the child's mind and the mother's. Even though we may suffer *yissurim* whose purpose escapes us, we trust that the loving Father would not harm us. We cannot understand the purpose of *yissurim* any more than an infant can understand immunization.

As a nation and as individuals, we have withstood many *yissurim*.

> *The tzaddik of Apta was once seen to be crying profusely. When asked why he was crying so, he said that he could foresee the agony that Jews would suffer before the Redemption. One of his chassidim tried to comfort him, saying, "Hashem will never give us more suffering than we can bear."*
>
> *The tzaddik's wept even more. "You don't know," he said, "how much suffering Jews can bear."*

⟫◈⟪

> *Zeide Reb Motele was away from home when he received the news that a fire had destroyed his library, in which there were irreplaceable manuscripts on Torah. For a few moments, he was sad, but then his cheerful demeanor returned and he said to his chassidim, "Why are you not asking for mashkeh [drinks]? The Talmud says that we must praise Hashem for the bad as well as the good. Had I come into a fortune, you would have asked for mashkeh to celebrate, so you should ask for mashkeh now, too."*
>
> *The chassidim said, "But we saw that the Rebbe was sad."*
>
> *Zeide Reb Motele said, "When Hashem gives us yissurim,*

we must feel the pain. After that, we should realize that it is for a good purpose."

The Talmud says that *yissurim* are a cleansing process, by which our sins are forgiven (*Berachos* 8a). While we believe this is so, we pray on Yom Kippur, "And what I have sinned before You, may You cleanse with Your abundant mercy, but not through suffering or serious illness." We attest to *yissurim* being a cleansing process, but we ask Hashem's mercy in sparing us from suffering.

What about the *tzaddikim* who welcomed suffering? Perhaps they wanted to *earn* forgiveness rather than to receive it as a Divine grace.

How could *tzaddikim* who were so holy and spiritual have considered themselves to be so sinful?

As I related in Four Chassidic Masters, R' Elimelech of Lizhensk would frequently fast and mortify himself to atone for his sins. One of his disciples who overheard him denouncing himself said, "How can the Master say things about himself that are untrue?"

R' Elimelech answered, "A king wanted to build a new palace, with all new furnishings and accessories. A peasant who was digging the foundation of the palace had a grudge against the king, and intentionally dug six meters in the wrong direction. When this was discovered, he was given 10 lashes, made to fill up the ditch, and dig in the right place.

"The jeweler who fashioned the diamond that was to be the centerpiece of the crown was a bit negligent and erred $1/10$ of a millimeter in cutting the stone. He was given a severe punishment and dismissed.

"The jeweler's unintentional deviation was $1/60{,}000$ that of the peasant, yet his punishment was much more severe. Why? Because when one is working with the centerpiece of the crown, there is no tolerance for even the slightest deviation."

Precisely because R' Elimelech was aware of his stature, he felt an infinitesimally small dereliction to be that much greater.

There are many *tzaddikim* who took very seriously the Talmudic statement that "sin begets sin" (*Ethics of the Fathers* 4:2).

One Shabbos, the Tzaddik of Rizhin rose from the table, and as he did so, he nudged the table a bit, inadvertently causing a candle to fall from the candlestick, thus extinguishing the flame. He cried inconsolably. When his children pointed out that this was clearly an accident, the Tzaddik said, "I am not concerned that the sin of the candle being extinguished was so grave, but even if it is minute, who knows what sins it can bring in its wake?" To the Tzaddik, even the minutest sin was akin to a single microscopic bacterium, which can reproduce and ultimately cause death.

A WORD OF ADVICE:

Know that even when we cannot fathom the purpose of our suffering, Hashem's love for us is boundless and His decrees are always for the good. We must recognize that suffering should bring about teshuvah.

15. Is This a Wake-up Call?

The financial meltdown struck us with the force of a tsunami. The impact is global. Could it be that this is a wake-up call, arousing us to re-evaluate our lifestyles? The world seems to have subscribed to the attitude of the 60's, "If it feels good, do it!" Except in those countries where there is frank starvation, it seems that pursuit of pleasure has become the goal in life.

As I mentioned, in my years of treating patients suffering from alcoholism, I have seen people experience many wake-up calls, which should have alerted them to the need to change their lifestyles. In some cases, the person was simply oblivious to the wake-up call. In others, there was a brief awareness, but soon thereafter it was forgotten.

I do not expect the secular world to recognize the financial meltdown as a wake-up call. At the very best, they may place the blame on people who were greedy or whose judgment was grossly impaired. Banks and corporations were reckless. Probably, few people think, *There is a message in this for me.*

Torah-abiding Jews believe in *hashgachah pratis* (Divine Providence), and we should be alert to hidden messages.

> *R' Zushe of Anipole was hurrying along the road when a peasant called to him, "Hey, you! Come help me unload this wagon."*
>
> *R' Zushe, who was hurrying to his destination, replied, "I can't."*
>
> *The man shouted back, "Yes, you can. You just don't want to."*
>
> *R' Zushe took this as a message from Heaven. When one thinks one is unable to do something, the truth may be that one just does not want to.*

Are we indeed living a Torah lifestyle? Yes, we have glatt-kosher meat, *chalav Yisrael*, *pas Yisrael*, we are meticulous in *shemiras Shabbos*, and our children receive the finest Torah education. What else should we be doing?

Ramban says that one can be meticulously observant of halachah, yet be far from *Yiddishkeit* (Jewish observance) (*Leviticus* 18:2). How can that be? A person may be indulgent in all halachically permissible pleasures, essentially living one's life according to a modified version of the 60's motto. Instead of, "If it feels good, do it!" one says, "If it feels good and is halachically permissible, do it!"

There is nothing wrong with enjoying life and having pleasure. Indeed, we will be asked on Judgment Day, "Did you enjoy My world?" The problem occurs when we allow pleasure to become the primary goal in life.

Mussar authorities point out that Torah was given to *mentschen* (people), not to animals. The distinguishing feature between man and animals is that man can have *middos* (fine character traits). A person who lacks *middos* fits the scientific appellation of *Homo sapiens*, which essentially means "an intelligent ape." While intelligence is indeed important, it is not man's primary identity. If it were, then the most intelligent person would be the finest human being, and we know that is not true. As we know, prior to World War II, the most intellectually advanced country was Germany.

The adoption of pursuit of pleasure as a goal in life is a relatively new phenomenon. Just 100 years ago, life was so full of hardships that one could not conceive of pleasure being one's ultimate goal. The average life expectancy was 40 years.

Infant mortality was high and childhood diseases were rampant. It was not unusual for a woman who had 10 pregnancies to remain with only three children who survived to adulthood.

Living conditions were far less comfortable than today. Work was often physically exhausting. Communication was difficult. On a hot, sweltering day, all one could do was sweat. There was no respite from wearying heat. I remember clothes being scrubbed by hand on a washboard and hung out to dry. We had an icebox rather than an electric refrigerator. Twice a week we had an ice delivery; the delivery man would carry huge blocks of ice up the stairs of the multistory walk-up buildings.

Today, things are radically different. We have automatic washing machines, dryers, and dishwashers. We can communicate anywhere around the world with a handheld cell phone. Journeying to Israel takes 10 hours instead of four weeks. On a hot day we are in cool comfort with air conditioning. Many foods are available as instant or frozen ready to be cooked, and microwave ovens have reduced cooking time from hours to minutes. Much work is done by electronic devices. One need not even ask for directions, because a GPS device will guide one every mile of the way to a destination.

These examples by no means exhaust the marvels of modern technology. With many of life's hardships eliminated, it is possible to think that life is intended to be used to attain all the pleasure one can.

Torah-observant people, too, are beneficiaries of modern technology. When I was a child, a slaughtered chicken had to be plucked, eviscerated, soaked, and salted. Gefilte fish required filleting the fish before grinding and chopping it. Today, both chicken and gefilte fish are available ready-for-the-pot. To drink *chalav Yisrael* we had to go to the farm at 5 a.m. to watch the milking. There were no *chalav Yisrael* dairy products. On Passover we ate potatoes, meat, potatoes, eggs, potatoes, apples, potatoes, and more potatoes. Today, everything except bread is available for Passover (yes, even kosher-for-Passover pizza!), and the largest counter in the store is loaded with of a variety of sweets and *nosherei*. There are glatt-kosher Chinese, Italian, and other ethnic foods and sushi. There are glatt-kosher cruises to exotic places in the world. With many hardships eliminated and many pleasures readily available, many Torah-observant people may be what Ramban referred to as being indulgent with a *hechsher* (rabbinical supervision).

Ramban makes a comment on the verse, "You shall be holy" (*Leviticus* 19:2): It is, therefore, a *d'Oraisa* (Biblical requirement) that we go beyond living a life with a *hechsher*.

What is it that we are to do over and above complying with halachah? Listen to the immortal words of Rambam in his Introduction to the Commentary on the Mishnah (emphasis added).

All animals and plants have only one or two tasks to fulfill. We see, for instance, that the date palms have nothing to do but bring forth dates, and accordingly so do all other trees. Furthermore, we find animals that only have to spin, like the spider; others, like the swallows, that build their nests in the summer; and animals that prey on other animals, like lions. But man has many different tasks. And they have examined all his activities in order to infer the purpose of his existence, and they found that he is preordained for only one activity, for the sake of which he was created, and that *he does everything else only to maintain his existence, so that he may carry out that one task. This sole task is to contemplate ideas in the soul and to know truth. Obviously, it is absurd to assume that man's purpose is to eat, drink, have physical satisfaction, build, for none of these things increases his essence; and, additionally, he has these things in common with most other creatures. It is wisdom that enhances Man's essence ... and the most sublime thought is when he contemplates in his soul the Oneness of G-d and associated G-dly thoughts.* The other sciences serve only for practice until one achieves the knowledge of G-d. ... Hence, the man who

> attains and exercises this knowledge *is achieving his purpose.*

We have here, in incomparable clarity and lucidity, the Torah concept of the purpose of man: "… to contemplate in his soul the Oneness of G-d." The Talmud states that Moses taught us 613 mitzvos (commandments). King David condensed them into 11 principles, Isaiah into six, Michah into three, and Habakkuk condensed them into a single principle, "The righteous will live with *emunah* (*Makkos* 23b). This is also Rambam's conclusion: contemplating the oneness of G-d.

Inasmuch as this is the purpose of our existence, how much time do we devote to this purpose? In the morning, in the evening, and upon retiring, we recite the verse, "Hear, O Israel, Hashem, our G-d, Hashem is the One and Only." Assuming that we think of the meaning of these words rather than reciting them by rote, many people devote a total of *15 seconds a day* to the purpose of their existence!

If we do not engage more diligently in contemplating the oneness of G-d and thereby fulfilling our purpose of existence, then what are we living for? Let us go back to Rambam, who continues:

> If Divine wisdom does not create anything in vain,
> if man is the most sublime of all creatures under

the moon and his purpose is to cultivate the higher cognition, why has G-d brought forth all the people who do not attain such knowledge? After all, we see that most people are without wisdom *and strive for pleasure*, and that the wise man who retreats from the world is rare among the many, occurring only once in an age. [The answer is:] All these people live in order to help this one man, for if all people aspired to wisdom and studied philosophy (and no one dealt with material things) then the world would not go on, and the species of man would perish.

Thus, there are two types of individuals. One type fulfills the purpose of his existence and enacts the purpose of the world, and the other enables the existence of these rare people by providing the needs for human existence. The function of the latter is essentially that of all other creations.

This is a chilling thought. There are relatively few people who contemplate the oneness of G-d. All the rest, who work in the fields, operate factories, teach the sciences, and practice their various professions are simply like the plants and animals that make Earth habitable for those who do contemplate the Oneness of G-d. If I do not contemplate the Oneness of G-d, I share a function with insects and grass. That is hardly edifying and does very little for my self-esteem.

This is a question every person should ask. "Do I wish to be merely an item in the world ecology, or do I wish to be someone who is enacting the purpose of the world?"

Perhaps the economic crisis is a wake-up call. Perhaps Hashem is seizing us by the lapels and giving us a thorough shaking, saying, "Look here, My dear child! You have been functioning far, far beneath your level. I created you to be superior to angels, yet you have chosen to exist on an animal level, albeit an intellectual animal. Wake up and begin living the life for which I designed you, and for which I instilled part of Myself, your *neshamah* within you!"

You may indeed realize that this is a wake-up call, but that is not yet enough.

> *I set my alarm clock to wake me at 5 a.m. When the alarm clock rings, I do what every normal person does; I turn it off and choose to sleep for just five minutes more. Usually, I wake up an hour later.*
>
> *One day, I had to catch an early-morning flight. I knew of my habit to turn off the alarm clock for just five more minutes of sleep, and realized that it might cause me to miss my flight. I took the alarm clock off the nightstand and put it in the far corner of the room so that I would not be able to turn it without getting out of bed. This enabled me to be at the airport in time for the flight.*

Wake-up calls may be like the alarm clock. Unless we take some action to avoid returning to our usual lifestyle, the wake-up call will not have accomplished anything.

What can we do? For a starter, let's increase the morning *davening* by just five minutes. It is surprising how these few minutes will allow us to concentrate on the words of the *tefillah*. Every morning, we should learn 15 minutes of *mussar* in addition to the *daf yomi*.

> *Someone asked R' Yisrael of Salant, inasmuch as he could spare only 15 minutes a day on Torah study, should he use this time to study Talmud or mussar? R' Yisrael told him to study mussar.*
>
> *"You mean that mussar takes precedence over Talmud?" the man asked.*
>
> *R' Yisrael said, "No, but if you learn mussar for 15 minutes, you will realize that you can make time for two hours study of Talmud."*

People pass by a *mezuzah* and perfunctorily touch it and kiss their fingertips. Rather than do that, pause for a few moments at the doorway and think of the words on the parchment contained in the *mezuzah*. Think about Rambam's words, "*A man achieves the most sublime idea when he contemplates in his soul the Oneness of G-d.*" That is a moment when you are fashioning yourself into what Hashem wanted you to be. That is a moment when you are "enacting the purpose of the world."

Perhaps we needed a wake-up call to make us think what it really means to be a Jew, children of the Patriarch Abraham, Avraham Avinu. It is generally accepted that he transformed the world. He was born into a pagan family that resided in a pagan environment. In fact, the entire world was pagan. *Echad hayah Avraham*, he was one, standing alone against the entire world. It is difficult to believe that in the entire world population there was not a single person other than Avraham Avinu who realized the folly of idolatry and that there can be only one G-d. How could reasonable people believe that those blocks of wood were gods?

An even more difficult question is posed as we see in the *Neviim* (Prophets) that the Jews in Eretz Yisrael worshiped idols, and that they were deaf to the reprimands of the prophets. How could this be? Why, after witnessing the miracles of the ten plagues, the splitting of the Reed Sea, the manna, the well of Miriam, and the Clouds of Glory, could the Jews still doubt Hashem, as is evident in the *Chumash* and especially in the episode of the spies? Am I to assume that people who, after seeing miracle after miracle, did not believe in Hashem, that they believed in statues? That is simply absurd!

Let's go back to the contribution of Avraham Avinu.

It was not just that he taught that there was only one G-d. The prevailing idea was *that a god was there to serve people.* Avraham Avinu developed the revolutionary concept of *avodas Hashem*. Man is to serve G-d, not the other way around.

If you hire someone to do a job for you and you are not pleased with his work, then you fire him and hire someone else. The Talmud in *Sanhedrin* explains that this is what *avodah zarah* was all about. "The Jews never believed that there was any substance to the idols, but because the Torah forbids certain relationships, they said, 'We'll get ourselves a god that says these relationships are permitted.'" And if G-d is there to serve our needs, this makes perfectly good sense.

That is what *avodah zarah* is. It is an attitude that "everything must please me." *Avodah zarah* rejects the idea that our existence is for something other than satisfying our own desires. Self-centeredness is self-worship, and that is *avodah zarah* whether or not one prays to idols.

Yes, we have many needs, and when these are not met, we suffer. But in *Tehillim* we say, "*betzaarasam Lo tzar* — when we suffer, Hashem suffers with us." The Talmud says that when Jews are in agony, the *Shechinah* says, "*Kalani meroshi kalani mezro'i* — My head is burdened, My arm is burdened" (*Sanhedrin* 46a). What we should be praying for is not our own comfort, but that Hashem should relieve our suffering for His sake.

A lumber merchant complained to a Rebbe that he stood to lose a great deal of money. He had bought a forest, but the price of lumber fell precipitously. The Rebbe said, "When you are in agony, it puts Hashem in agony. Is it worthwhile to cause Hashem to suffer because of a few pieces of wood?"

Why, then, are there so many *tefillos* for our personal needs? It is to impress upon us our utter dependence on Hashem, so that we do not deviate from His instructions in the Torah. These were given for *our* benefit, but because the *yetzer hara* tries to blind us to this, we must be constantly reminded of it.

Perhaps the wake-up call is meant to direct our attention to the fact that we have lost sight that so much of our lives is self-centered. This concept has a very important application to our personal lives, particularly to family life, to our roles as husbands and wives and as parents. Jewish family life has suffered great setbacks. Never before have there been so many divorces among the Torah-observant population. Never before have there been so many problems with children who are not respectful of their parents and with children who leave *Yiddishkeit*.

The ultimate factor generally responsible for the epidemic of divorces is that spouses are disappointed and frustrated because their spouses are not meeting *their* expectations and not adequately satisfying *their* needs. Too many marriages are based on the expectation that one's spouse will gratify all one's needs. One generally does not enter into marriage because it will give one the opportunity to *give* to another person, but rather because one expects to receive what one wants from another person. Marriages that are based on the need to give rather than to receive are not as likely to result in frustration and disappointment.

Chazal tried to convey this message through the *berachos* that are recited under the *chuppah* (wedding canopy). The first *berachah* is *shehakol bara lichvodo* — everything was created to bring glory to Hashem. The primary purpose of the marriage is to establish a family that will increase *kevod Shamayim*, and while it is, of course, important that one's personal needs be met, these are secondary to the foundation of the marriage. In a marriage based on *shehakol bara lichvodo*, if there is any personal frustration, it does not attack and undermine the basis of the marriage, and if the foundation of the marriage remains intact, these secondary issues can and will be resolved.

Some will say that this concept is too lofty for us mere mortals. Well, the second of the seven *berachos* is *yotzer haadam* — Hashem created man. One might ask, "What is the relevance of this *berachah* to the marriage?"

Prior to creation of man, Hashem created a myriad of living things, great and small. Although there are vast differences among animals, there is one characteristic common to all of them. Animals, except for domesticated pets that may adopt human traits, are motivated solely by self-gratification. Animals cannot be altruistic. Animals cannot do acts of *chesed*. Man was created with the unique ability to be motivated by something other than self-gratification. If a person cannot go beyond his own skin to do *chesed*, he is essentially functioning at an animal level. He may have multiple degrees and be highly intelligent, he may be a brilliant scientist, an accomplished philosopher, or a virtuoso, but if he is self-centered, he has not advanced beyond the animal stage and is indeed what science calls him, *Homo sapiens,* an ape with intellect.

One who wishes to participate in enacting the purpose of the world realizes that in order for a marriage to be successful, one must become a being who does *chesed*, who considers others, rather than just oneself, and *the place where this begins is in the relationship between husband and wife.* Certainly every person has needs, but one's own needs should be secondary to the needs of the spouse. Only in this way can there be true love, a dignified love that is unique to humans.

In his epochal essay "*Chesed uNesinah,*" R' Dessler points out the fallacy in the popular concept that "you give to those whom you love," and points out that just the reverse is true;

"you love those to whom you give." In the kabbalah writings, *ahavah* is identified with *chesed*. True love in a marriage is when both partners are primarily motivated by consideration of the other's needs rather than their own. That is why the Sages formulated the *berachah yotzer haadam*, telling the young couple that a happy and enduring marriage requires remembering that one is an *adam*, distinguished from other living creatures not merely by intelligence, but by the ability to be motivated by *chesed* rather than self-centeredness.

As I said, *chesed* must begin in the husband-wife relationship. Heed the words of R' Chaim Vital, the disciple of the Arizal.

> A person may have performed many acts of *chesed* throughout his lifetime, and been of great help to many people. When he leaves this world, he is secure in his belief that the *Beis Din shel Maalah*, the Heavenly Tribunal, will open the gates of Gan Eden wide, and a host of angels will escort him to a high place in Gan Eden, where he will receive his well-deserved rich reward. How shocked he will be to find that the gates of Gan Eden are tightly shut before him; no angels, no rich reward. He will protest, "Where is justice? Where is the reward for my life long devotion to *chesed?*"

The Heavenly Tribunal will say, "We observed your behavior at home. You did not act with *chesed* toward your wife. You were inconsiderate of her feelings and her needs. You spoke disrespectfully to her. You became angry at her when she did not fulfill your wants. In the absence of *chesed* at home, all the *chesed* that you did outside of the house is of no merit."

Think of it! The great mitzvah of *gemilas chassadim* is meritorious only if one behaves with *chesed* at home.

Avraham Avinu came upon a world population that was totally self-centered. Relationships between people were totally selfish, resulting in the decadence of the generation of the *Mabul* (Flood), the arrogance of the generation of the Tower of Babel, and the corruption of Sodom and Amorah. Their religion was essentially self-worship, and their gods were there to serve them, to please them.

Avraham Avinu reasoned that this could not be why Hashem had endowed man with so great a mind. If self-centeredness is the desired theme of life, then man would have been better off with the mind of a cow, because the minds of cows are much better suited to self-gratification and contentment than the minds of humans. Cows do not have anxiety and emotional problems. Give them grass and a place to rest, and they are content. Man was given a mind that makes him capable of going beyond the animalistic needs of the body. Avraham Avinu was unique in promulgating *avodas Hashem* and *chesed*, both going beyond one's personal desires and needs. That was the contribution of Avraham Avinu.

A home in which the relationships between parents are characterized by *chesed*, in which there is a wholesome *shalom bayis*, is one that children are not likely to reject. It is tragic when a child goes off the *derech* and leaves *Yiddishkeit*. There may be various reasons why this happens, but there is a Yiddish aphorism, "*fun kein guts antloift men nisht* — one does not run away from something that is pleasant." Numerous children who are off the *derech* say that they were disappointed in the *Yiddishkeit* they observed; although there may have been strict observance of the mitzvos, there was also a lack of Torah *middos* (character traits). The kabbalah writers say that although there are a number of positive *middos*, *chesed* is an ingredient in all of them.

Even strict justice must be leavened with *chesed*, especially when dealing with one's children. *Gevurah* is a stern *middah,* and it is often necessary to exercise *gevurah* (lit., strength) in disciplining children. Children accept discipline when it is done with true love; even if they are momentarily angry at being disciplined, they eventually realize that it was done out of love for them. This is referred to as *gevurah shebechesed.*

However, if a parent goes into rage for whatever reason, that is incompatible with *chesed*. If children see self-centeredness in parents who are Torah observant, they may lose respect for Torah.

Self-centeredness is the antithesis of Torah. In describing the revelation at Sinai, Moses said, "*Anochi omeid bein Hashem uveineichem* — I stood between Hashem and you" (*Deuteronomy* 5:5) One of the Chassidic rebbeim said that this verse also has another meaning: *anochi*, the *I*, the ego, is what stands between Hashem and you. The ego is a barrier between man and Hashem. When the *sifrei mussar* refer to *bittul*, or self-effacement, they are referring to eliminating self-centeredness. It is only with self-effacement that we elevate ourselves to a level above animals and act in accordance with the precepts of Avraham Avinu.

Our generation may have been in need of a wake-up call, painful as it may be. We know that the worst feature of deadly diseases is that they may not produce any symptoms until the disease is far advanced. Early pain may save a person's life. Perhaps today's crisis is the pain that will call our attention to whether we are indeed preserving the legacy of Avraham Avinu.

We must realize that the wake-up call is intended to inspire us to mend our ways and focus on developing the middos that will enable us to live our lives with full bitachon and emunah in Hashem.

16. Responding to the Wake-up Call: Living With a Purpose

The *sefarim* say that serving Hashem is not limited to performance of the mitzvos. Eating, sleeping, and engaging in work and business can all be *avodas Hashem*.

> The Baal Shem Tov prayed that it be revealed to him who will be his companion in Gan Eden. When he was told who it was, he traveled to see that person. He was surprised to see

that the man was a simple, rather unlearned person. The Baal Shem Tov observed him closely to see what it was that made him so virtuous. He found nothing unusual, other than that the man ate voraciously. The Baal Shem Tov asked him, "Why do you eat so much? Are you really that hungry?"

"No," the man said, "I must force myself to eat. You see, years ago, my father was accosted by a band of rogues, who forced him to kiss a crucifix. He was a weak man, and when he refused, they beat him mercilessly until he finally lost his life. But I am eating to make myself strong so if that ever happens to me, I will be able to whip them."

The Baal Shem Tov said that he now understood this person's great merit. "Every morsel of food he ate was for kiddush Hashem [santification of G-d's name]."

If one eats to have the energy to learn Torah and do mitzvos, each morsel can be a mitzvah.

The Midrash relates that when the Patriarch Jacob, Yaakov Avinu, left home at his parents' bidding to go to Lavan, he stopped off at the academy of Shem and Eber and studied Torah for 14 years, during which he never had a sound night's sleep. On his way from the academy to Lavan, Yaakov Avinu slept at the site of the future *Beis HaMikdash* (Holy Temple), and dreamt of angels ascending and descending to and from Heaven, and he heard Hashem speak to him.

Upon awakening he said, "Surely Hashem is present in this place, and I did not know" (*Genesis* 28:10-16). One of the Chassidic rebbes said, "What was it that Yaakov Avinu did not know? During his 14 years with Shem and Eber he did not sleep, because he did not want to be idle from Torah study. Now he discovered that in sleep one can dream of angels and hear Hashem. 'I did not know that one can do *avodas Hashem* with sleep.'"

If one sleeps to be rested so that he can be alert to Torah study, *tefillah,* and performance of mitzvos, sleep becomes *avodas Hashem.*

If one engages in work or business to earn the means to provide children with a Torah *chinuch* (education), to support Torah institutions, to give *tzeddakah*, and to acquire the necessities for mitzvos, then engaging in work and business becomes *avodas Hashem*.

Although Rambam said, "It is absurd to assume that man's purpose is to eat, drink, have physical satisfaction, build houses, or be a ruler, for none of these things increases his essence; after all, he has these things in common with all other creatures," these activities can be taken out of the animal level and elevated to a uniquely human level, which befits the dignity of man.

Perhaps the wake-up call is to dedicate everything we do to *avodas Hashem*.

Eventually, the economy will recover and our lives will stabilize. It is then that we must remember to give real meaning to our lives.

Perhaps the economic crisis is a wake-up call to direct our attention to the fact that so much of our lives is self-centered. Hashem wants us to up the ante and be all we can possible be, all that He intended us to be.

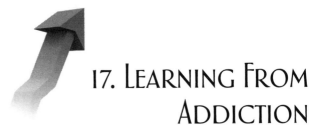

17. Learning From Addiction

The past 40 years of working with addicts has taught me a great deal about human nature. I wrote *Addictive Thinking*, which describes how an addict's thought process works. We may readily recognize the bizarre thinking of the alcoholic or drug addict, who is totally oblivious to the ruination resulting from his habit, and he can present his case in a quasi-logical manner, sometimes succeeding in deceiving others as well as himself.

I was not aware of it at the time, but my first lesson in addiction was given to me by my mother when I was 6 years old. One of the bedtime stories she told me was about a poor man, a beggar who prayed to Hashem for wealth. One day, he awoke to find a purse near his bed. He opened the purse and found a dollar in it. When he removed the dollar, another dollar appeared in its place, and he joyfully continued pulling out dollar after dollar. After several days, he was found starved to death, lying on a huge pile of dollars. It was a long while before I understood the moral of this story.

There is never enough alcohol for the alcoholic, never enough heroin or cocaine for the drug addict, never enough money for the workaholic. How much does this really differ from the comment of the multibillionaire, J. Paul Getty, who was asked, "How much money is enough?" Getty replied, "Just a little more."

I have had some exceedingly wealthy people as patients, and I asked them why they were aggressively pursuing more money, inasmuch as they could not possibly use up a fraction of their wealth if they lived for a thousand years. They frankly answered, "It is the thrill of making more money." They admitted that they have no use for the money, but are pursuing the "high" of acquisition. I see this as basically no different from the behavior of a drug addict who pursues a chemical high. Granted, it is not as physically destructive as drugs and may not lead to frankly criminal behavior (although it may lead to white-collar crime, as witnessed by the recent scandal involving someone who bilked people out of $50 billion), but the senseless accumulation of money is out of control; hence, it qualifies as an addiction.

It is not only the multibillionaires who have fallen into this addiction. This is also true of less wealthy people whose pursuit of wealth or the involvement in their business has become the primary motivation in their lives. The similarity to the addict is that they do not recognize that they have lost control of their lives. Many people are unaware that they have lost their freedom and are slaves to the office instead of being its masters.

The common denominator of addictions is "loss of control," whether it involves alcohol, food, drugs, gambling, shopping, Internet, or attachment to the office. Some people are able to go on vacation and arrange that the office contact them only in case of a true emergency. Others will be tied to their beeper or cell phone, and call the office four times a day. In the latter case, it is not that the office needs them, but they who need the office.

Addiction is a complex condition, probably the result of a combination of multiple causes. One of the factors is learned behavior. If a child sees loss of control in a parent, the child may be predisposed to engage in an addictive behavior. The parent who is addicted to the office or to making money may be teaching addictive behavior to the child.

We have the responsibility of providing our children with *chinuch*.

Chinuch is not limited to education. *Chinuch* means "training" and "preparation"; just as we immunize our children to prevent them from serious illnesses, we must prepare them for dealing with adversity. While we hope that they will never suffer adversity, it is unrealistic to think that it cannot happen, and they should not be unprepared. The Talmud says that a father should teach his son how to swim. Of course, the father hopes that the son will never be on a boat that capsizes, but because it is within the realm of possibility, he should be able to save himself.

Our lives are replete with ups and downs. It is rare, if not impossible, for a person to go through a lifetime without experiencing any adversity. A child may encounter adversity in grade school. How is he to deal with that? How is he to know that failing to be promoted to fifth grade is not the end of the world? How is he to know that being disappointed in a *shidduch* of which he was very hopeful is no reason to give up on life?

I have worked with many an alcoholic whose life was a disaster, but he or she recovered. I tell them that the most precious gift they have given their children is the fact that they are living examples of how a person can survive adversity and be happy.

There are many things that cannot be learned well at school. The rebbi may teach the children the Talmud that says, "Who is wealthy? He who is happy with his lot" (*Ethics of the Fathers* 4:1). If the children see that the parents are happy with what they have, they will accept the Talmudic teaching. If they see that the parents are depressed because they lost money, they will dismiss the Talmudic teaching as untrue, and set their goal as pursuit of riches, assuming that only wealth can bring happiness.

A WORD OF ADVICE:

This is what we can do now. The children should be made aware of the impact of the economic crisis, and they should see how adults are coping with it, even managing to smile and enjoy what is enjoyable. They cannot learn this in any school, only at home.

18. *Emunah, Bitachon,* and *Hishtadlus*

Fulfilling the commandments of putting on *tefillin,* eating matzah, and sitting in the *succah* are quite easy. Truly having *emunah* and *bitachon* are without doubt the most difficult, yet the most fundamental elements of Torah observance. These concepts are widely discussed in the works of *Mussar* and *Chassidus,* yet their parameters are difficult to understand and apply.

It is of interest that the need for strengthening one's *emunah* and *bitachon* in Hashem gains in importance in times of economic crisis, but relatively little thought is given to them when one has job security and one's financial investments are doing well. When economic conditions are stable, people may think that this is a natural state. Paychecks are received on time and stock values increase or decrease with the level of performance of the various companies. Everything is proceeding in an orderly fashion according to the laws of economics, which are considered rather similar to the law of gravity. If someone throws an object into the air, it will return to the ground because of the principle of gravity, and one usually does not consider that Hashem created the law of gravity and thereby caused the object to fall. Similarly, profit and loss and the orderly fluctuations in the economy are the results of the laws of economics, apparently without Hashem's direct involvement.

This is really no different from our attitude toward our physical functioning. True, we do recite the morning *berachos* thanking Hashem for the ability to arise and move about, but these are rather perfunctory. Some people may not seek Hashem's participation unless they are unable to function normally; should disease or injury occur, one's prayers are recited with greater intensity. If, G-d forbid, disease causes paralysis of an arm or leg, one will pray fervently to Hashem to restore it to its previous condition, as though His help to move the arm or leg is not needed when one is in good health.

R' Moshe Teitelbaum, author of Yismach Moshe, received a dowry from his father-in-law, and entrusted it to someone to invest for him. Unfortunately, the investment failed, and the Yismach Moshe was left destitute, but he continued his Torah study under those difficult circumstances.

One day, as he was studying Torah, the thought occurred to him that if he were somehow able to obtain a significant sum of money, he would give it to someone more reliable to invest for him, and he would be able to devote himself to Torah study with peace of mind.

As he was thinking this, a deep sleep came over him, and he dreamed that he was in Gan Eden. He walked from one hall to another, until he came to one hall where a tzaddik was teaching Torah. The tzaddik shone brightly, and each word seemed to be aflame.

"Who is this tzaddik?" the Yismach Moshe asked.

"That is the holy Arizal," he was told.

The Yismach Moshe trembled in awe. Then he heard the tzaddik call to him, "Young man! If a person had 10,000 talents of silver, would he not be dependent on the compassion of Hashem? Inasmuch as a person is always dependent on Hashem, what difference does it make whether one has 1 gulden or 10,000 gulden?"

Torah literature stresses that nothing occurs without

Hashem's participation, and that there is really no difference between natural and miraculous phenomena, other than that natural phenomena are regular and predictable, whereas miracles do not follow any laws of nature. However, Hashem's participation in the development of an apple seed into a fruit-bearing tree is no less miraculous than His dividing the Reed Sea. The fact that the laws of nature are regular and orderly gives the appearance that they are operating independent of Hashem, but this is a misperception. Nature is nothing other than a series of ongoing miracles. Hashem is at the helm of everything that occurs in the world.

Two pranksters went to Yellowstone National Park, to which millions of people come to witness the eruption of Old Faithful. This natural geyser has been erupting at set intervals since time immemorial. The pranksters brought a huge steering wheel and shaft from a junkyard, and placed the shaft into the ground on a hill near the geyser, where they would be seen by the tourists. The park guide explained the geyser phenomenon to the tourists, and said that the geyser would shortly erupt ....

Just as the geyser was about to erupt, one prankster shouted to the other, "Okay! Let 'er go!" The other prankster gave the wheel a vicious turn, and the geyser erupted.

Understandably, the tourists may have believed that the

*natural eruption of Old Faithful was a fabrication, and was
really caused by the release of a valve.*

Appearances can be deceptive. The sun rising in the east
every day is a "natural" phenomenon, the lake freezing in
subzero weather is a "natural" phenomenon, and economic
cycles are "natural" phenomena. Torah literature teaches
that except for the moral choice between good and evil,
which Hashem has left to man's free will, Hashem controls
everything. Ramban (*Exodus* 13:16) says that nature is a series
of miracles in which the hand of Hashem is concealed. Even
the "automatic" is on "manual."

The relevance of this concept to one's economic status is
in the words of Moses, "And you may say in your heart, 'My
strength and the might of my hand made me all this wealth!'
Then you shall remember Hashem, that it was He Who gave
you strength to make wealth" (*Deuteronomy* 8:17).

People who are asked, "Do you have *emunah*?" will
invariably say, "Of course, I believe in Hashem."

"And do you have *bitachon*?" That is not as certain. The
Gaon of Vilna said that "the primary purpose of giving the
Torah to Israel was for them to have *bitachon* in Hashem,
because *bitachon* encompasses all the mitzvos" (*Gra, Proverbs*
22:19).

Just what is *bitachon*? Some people think that *bitachon* in

Hashem means that He will conduct things so that everything will turn out the way one wishes. That is a mistake. We have no guarantee that Hasherm will do what we want. Indeed, we may not understand that what we want is not for our ultimate good.

Bitachon means to believe that nothing ever occurs without Hashem's will that it be so. There are no "natural" occurrences that Hashem did not will to happen. And *bitachon* means believing that what Hashem causes to happen is just, even though we cannot possibly understand how it can be so. *Bitachon* means believing that when it pleases Hashem, He can suspend the laws of nature, resulting in what we see as a miracle.

Our *sefarim* tell us that how much a person will earn during the year is preordained on Rosh Hashanah, and that one cannot increase one's earnings beyond that amount. That is a principle of *emunah*. This brings up the thorny issue of *hishtadlus* versus *bitachon*. What purpose is there in a person working and exerting himself to earn, if what one is destined to earn will be his anyway?

> *In Belz, a local doctor complained to the Belzer Rebbe, "Why is it that you send the poor patients to me, and the wealthy patients you send to Lvov or to Vienna? Are only the big city doctors permitted to earn large fees?"*

The Rebbe answered, "On Rosh Hashanah, not only is how much money a person will earn that year preordained, but the amount of money he will pay to doctors is also preordained. For the person who earns little, the amount that is preordained that he will spend on doctors is small, and is quickly exhausted when you treat them. For the wealthy person, a much larger sum that he will pay doctors is preordained. If you were to treat him, he would have to be ill a long time to use up the preordained amount, so I send him to the big city where that amount will be used up quickly, so he will not have to be ill for long."

Some Torah commentaries say that had Adam not sinned, all his needs would have been provided for him and he would have been free to contemplate the Oneness of Hashem all day. As a result of his sin, he was cursed, "By the sweat of your brow shall you eat bread" (*Genesis* 3:19). They point out that inasmuch as the decree that man must work for a livelihood was a curse, it would seem logical that a person would want to minimize the curse, rather than devoting the lion's share of the day to it.

The *sefarim* say that although a person is required to do something to earn a livelihood, that does not mean that his preordained earnings will come from any specific things he does. He may think that his earnings derive from his efforts in doing "A," whereas they may come from an altogether different source.

> *The Baal Shem Tov's disciples asked him how one can reconcile two contradictory statements in the Talmud. One statement is that a person's earnings are preordained on Rosh Hashanah (Beitzah 16a). On the other hand, the Talmud says that a person's lot is judged daily (Rosh Hashanah 16a). Which statement is correct?*
>
> *The Baal Shem Tov looked out the window and saw Chaikel, the water carrier. He summoned him and asked, "Nu, Chaikel, how are things with you?"*
>
> *Chaikel sighed. "Not good, Rebbe," he said. "At my age, I have to make my living by shlepping heavy buckets of water."*
>
> *A few days later, the Baal Shem Tov again saw Chaikel carrying buckets of water. "Nu, how is it with you?" he asked.*
>
> *Chaikel smiled, "Rebbe," he said, "if at my age I can still shlep buckets of water, I can't complain. Thank G-d for this."*
>
> *The Baal Shem Tov told his disciples, "Both Talmudic statements are true. On Rosh Hashanah, it was decreed that Chaikel will earn his livelihood as a water carrier. How Chaikel accepts his lot, that varies from day to day."*

R' Levi Yitzchak of Berditchev once stopped a man who was hurrying through the marketplace. "I'm sorry, Rebbe," the man said. "I am in a hurry to get my parnassah [livelihood]."

R' Levi Yitzchak said, "How can you be so sure that your parnassah lies in the direction toward which you are heading? Maybe it is in the opposite direction, and you are actually running away from it!"

⸻

It is related that one Friday morning the Baal Shem Tov knocked on someone's door and left. When the person opened the door and saw no one there, he looked down the road and saw a man in the distance. He went after him and asked, "Did you knock on my door?"

The Baal Shem Tov said, "Yes."

"Then why did you walk away? What did you want from me?"

The Baal Shem Tov replied, "I did not want anything from you. I am required to make a hishtadlus [do an action] to get bread for Shabbos, and my knocking on your door was that action. But that does not mean that you are the one who is to provide for me."

The consensus appears to be that the amount of *hishtadlus* a person should put forth varies with one's spirituality and with the strength and sincerity of his *emunah* and *bitachon*. Pursuant to this concept are the following two stories, which reflect a degree of *emunah* and *bitachon* that may be beyond our reach. Then why tell them? It is like the story of the violin student whose father took him to a concert by the great violinist, Itzhak Perlman. When they left, the father said, "Do you think you will ever be able to play like that?"

The son said, "No, but I'm going to practice an extra half-hour every day."

Stories about perfection may motivate us to increase our efforts.

The Baal Shem Tov was directed to a certain person who had achieved absolute bitachon in Hashem. The Baal Shem Tov went to meet him, and asked to stay with him for a few days so that he could learn from him.

The man told the Baal Shem Tov that he earned his livelihood by operating a flour mill that he rented from the local poritz. The yearly rental was 1,000 rubles, and the due date was the next day.

"Do you have the thousand rubles?" the Baal Shem Tov asked.

"No," the man said. "I don't have even 10 rubles."

"Are you going to borrow the money?" "No," the man said. "There is no one from whom I can borrow."

"Then how do you plan to pay the poritz?" the Baal Shem Tov asked.

"That is Hashem's problem, not mine," the man said.

The Baal Shem Tov saw that the man was in a cheerful mood, going about his business as if he had not a single worry.

Later that day, a representative from the poritz arrived. "Do you have the rent money?" he asked.

The man answered, "Why are you bothering me today? The rent is not due until tomorrow."

"Very well," the representative said, "but just remember, the poritz does not deal kindly with tenants who do not pay the rent on time."

"Go away," the man said.

The following day, the Baal Shem Tov asked, "How are you going to get 1,000 rubles today?"

The man answered, "I told you yesterday, that is Hashem's worry, not mine."

At noontime, the poritz's representative came to collect the rent. The man said, "I am not in arrears until the day is over. Don't bother me."

The representative said, "You can expect a harsh reaction if you don't pay the rent. The poritz may have you flogged, tear down your house, and/or imprison you in the dungeon." The man did not appear the least bit worried.

That afternoon, three grain merchants stopped at the mill. "We want to buy the grain from all the poritz's farms. We know that you have dealings with him, and we want to engage you to negotiate for us."

"I'll be glad to," the man said. "My fee is 1,000 rubles."

"A thousand rubles?" the merchant said. "Have you gone mad? Fifty rubles is the most we will pay."

"Then go to the poritz yourself or buy the grain elsewhere," the man said. "My fee is a thousand rubles, nothing less."

The merchants left angrily, The Baal Shem Tov noticed that the man's cheerful disposition had not changed.

About an hour before sunset, the poritz's representative came again. "Now is your last chance to pay the rent," he said.

The man said, "Come in and wait a while. It is still an hour to sunset.'

A bit later the three merchants made an appearance. "We've looked elsewhere to buy grain, but we found nothing. Here is 1,000 rubles to negotiate for us with the poritz."

The man took the money and said, "Come with me to the poritz," and invited the representative to join him.

The Baal Shem Tov said, "Now I know what it means to have bitachon in Hashem." Even the Baal Shem Tov felt that *he needed to improve his bitachon.*

———◆———

Another story is told about Rabbi Yeshaya Horowitz (Shelah HaKadosh, 1558–1628), who delivered a Shabbos sermon in which he said that a person's earnings are determined on Rosh Hashanah, and that if a person would have absolute trust in Hashem, he would not have to work. His parnassah will come to him.

The Shelah's sister was married to a very simple, pious man, who made a living as a porter, delivering merchandise with his horse and wagon. On Sunday, after returning from services and eating breakfast, the man took the book of Psalms and leisurely began reciting the psalms.

"Why aren't you going out to work?" his wife said.

"I don't have to work," the man said. "The Rabbi said that Hashem will provide for me."

"The Rabbi did not mean for you to sit and do nothing," the wife said.

"I am not doing 'nothing,'" the man said. "I am reciting the psalms."

The wife went to the Shelah's home. "My dear brother," she said, "you must be careful what you say in your sermons. My husband refuses to go to work. He says that Hashem will provide for him."

"If he is really sincere in his trust in Hashem," the Shelah said, "Hashem will indeed provide for him."

Later that day, a man came to the door. He saw a horse and wagon near the house, and asked if they were for hire. The husband lent him the horse and wagon.

This man was a highwayman, who had robbed and murdered those from whom he had stolen. He had buried the loot, and now planned to retrieve it. He dug deeply for the loot and loaded it on the wagon. When he descended into the pit once more to check if he had overlooked any of his ill-gotten gains, the walls caved in, burying him.

As time passed, the horse became hungry, and familiar with the paths, found its way back to its owner's dwelling. The husband was the beneficiary of the robber's loot.

When the Shelah learned of this, he said, "It is not enough to just express trust in Hashem. This man's trust was absolute. He believed wholeheartedly that Hashem would provide for him, and his trust was so profound that he sincerely believed that he already possessed what Hashem had predetermined for him. That is the kind of trust in Hashem that is effective."

Since most of us cannot aspire to so lofty a level of *bitachon*, we are caught in the quandary of *hishtadlus* versus *bitachon*. After doing considerable research, a person purchases merchandise and sells it at a legitimate markup, earning a profit. It is only natural that he may feel that his business acumen and effort resulted in his earning the profit. He should remember, however, that "It was He Who gave you the judgment to acquire possessions."

R' Dessler has an excellent essay on the subject in *Michtav M'Eliyahu* (Vol.1, pp. 187-203), and points out that it is very difficult to avoid thinking that it is one's *hishtadlus* that brought about the result. He recommends that a person pray with great *kavannah* to achieve the awareness that the success or failure of one's *hishtadlus* is totally dependent on Hashem's *hashgachah*. One should also study the *sefarim* to strengthen one's *bitachon*, and one should seek to cut back on the time one spends in work and leisure and maximize the time one devotes to Torah-study. The additional Torah-study time should first be taken by reducing time spent on nonessential activities, and then one may be able to reduce the time at work for the sake of Torah study.

One must be careful not to justify indolence on the grounds of *bitachon*. If we have not achieved the sincere *bitachon* of the *Shelah's* brother-in-law, we may not relax in leisure and expect that Hashem will provide for our needs. Laziness is not *bitachon*.

R' Dessler asks, "Since Hashem preordains a person's earnings, why did He make *hishtadlus* necessary at all?"

R' Dessler cites R' Simchah Zissel, who states that *hishtadlus* is one of the *nisyonos* (trials) given to man. Ramchal in Chapter 1 of *Mesillas Yesharim* says, "The Holy One, Blessed is He, has put man in a place where the factors that draw him further from the Blessed One are many. These are the earthly desires which, if he is pulled after them, cause him to be drawn further from and to depart from the true good. It is seen, then, that man is veritably placed in the midst of a raging battle. For all the affairs of the world, whether for the good or for the bad, are trials to a man."

R' Simchah Zissel says that this is one of the most difficult trials to which a person is subjected. It is relatively easier to refrain from yielding to a forbidden desire. It is much more difficult to deny one's senses in favor of one's *emunah*. Hashem conceals Himself under the cloak of nature, as it were, so that people can mistake His providential acts as being "natural," and they fail to recognize the hand of Hashem in everything.

R' Simchah Zissel further states that prior to Adam's sin, he had a clear awareness that everything is wrought by Hashem. The immediate hand of Hashem in all that transpired was evident. The sin of eating from the Tree of Knowledge brought Adam and mankind to an awareness of nature, so that one may fail to ascribe everything to Hashem. The trial of *hishtadlus* is thus to undo the effects of Adam's transgression, which is accomplished when a person rejects the idea that it is his *hishtadlus* that earns his livelihood, and instead realizes that it is the hand of Hashem that accomplishes this.

We can reinforce our *bitachon* when we read the story of Joseph. What could be worse than being torn away from a doting father, sold into slavery, and falsely imprisoned for years? Yet, when, after Jacob's death, Joseph's brothers sought his forgiveness for fear that he would now take revenge for their cruelty toward him, Joseph said, "Fear not, for am I instead of G-d? Although you intended me harm, G-d intended it for good: in order to accomplish — it is as clear as this day — that a vast people be kept alive" (*Genesis* 50:19-20). Joseph bore them no grudge because to him it was "as clear as this day" that all that happened to him was Hashem manipulating things for His purpose. Indeed, he saw his brothers as merely being the tools whereby Hashem executed His plan.

Another lesson from the Joseph saga can be derived from the Torah statement that the Ishmaelite caravan to which Joseph was sold was carrying "spices, balsam, and lotus" to sell in Egypt (*Genesis* 37:25). Rashi cites the Midrash that the Ishmaelites usually transported foul-smelling goods, but in order to spare Joseph from that offensive odor, Hashem arranged that this caravan be the exception that carried fragrant spices.

The Torah commentaries ask: Joseph was kidnapped and sold as a slave. Was it important that the odor to which he was exposed be pleasant? In the broad scheme of things, this is relatively trivial. They answer: This indicates the precision of Hashem's judgment. Joseph was punished for having spoken *lashon hara* (defamatory talk) about his brothers (*Rashi, Genesis* 37:2), and was therefore sold into slavery. That was the just punishment that Hashem had decreed, but there was not to be even an iota of unpleasantness beyond that. There was no decree that he be exposed to offensive odors, and Hashem, therefore, arranged that he be spared from that unpleasantness.

A sincere, firm *emunah* in Hashem can make the most trying circumstances tolerable.

A WORD OF ADVICE:

Having sincere emunah and bitachon in the belief that everything — no matter how trivial — is wrought solely by the hand of Hashem enables one to accept his present state with equanimity. One will then come to the realization that the amount of hishtadlus necessary depends on one's level of spirituality and on the strength and sincerity of one's emunah and bitachon.

19. EMUNAH AND YISSURIM

As was noted, it is difficult for us to fully understand *yissurim*, yet we should see what our great Torah scholars said about the subject.

We should be aware that even when a person complains about *yissurim*, claiming that he feels Hashem is unfair and that he is being punished unjustly, that person has great *emunah*. He obviously believes in Hashem and that Hashem is in full control of the world, because if he did not believe it, he could not think of Hashem as being unfair. He may actually have a greater degree of *emunah* than people who have not experienced *yissurim* and may not have given serious thought to Hashem's *hashgachah*.

While some explanations of *yissurim* are given in the Talmud, they are greatly reinforced by *tzaddikim* closer to our own times, and of whose greatness we have evidence. We have been eyewitnesses to *tzaddikim* who lived what they taught, and although we may not reach their level of *kedushah*, nevertheless, they authenticate the teachings of the Talmud for us.

Eyewitnesses report that the Chofetz Chaim (d. 1933), upon the death of his son, said, "*Ribono shel Olam* [Master of the Universe]! The love that I can no longer give my son, I give to You!"

The daughter of his contemporary, Rabbi Avraham David Rabinowitz Thumim (Aderet), passed away. Although he was known to always be punctual, he was late arriving at her funeral. He explained, "The Talmud says that one must recite the *berachah* 'Baruch Dayan Emes' [Blessed is the True Judge] praising Hashem when one has suffered misfortune, and that one must say this *berachah* with his whole heart [*Berachos* 54a]. At first, I was unable to say this *berachah* wholeheartedly, so I had to meditate and contemplate Hashem's compassion until I was able to do so."

R' Yisrael of Rizhin was the victim of an anti-Semitic plot, and when he was imprisoned, he cited the verse, "Princes have pursued me without cause, but my heart has feared Your utterance. I rejoice over Your word, like one who finds abundant spoils" (Psalms 119:161-162). R' Yisrael said, "When I was first taken to prison, I was not upset that I was being persecuted innocently by princes, but I was worried that it was Your decree that I be jailed. Then I rethought it and said, 'If it was Your word that it be so, then I rejoice over Your will.'"

───➤◦◄───

Tzaddikim genuinely believed in the benevolence of yissurim. R' Baruch of Medzhibozh was reciting the prayer before Kiddush Friday night, and when he came to the words, "I gratefully thank You, Hashem, my G-d and G-d of my forefathers, for all the kindness You have done with me, and which You will do with me," he paused. "Why do I have to thank Hashem for the kindness that He will do with me in the future? I can thank Him at that time."

After a few moments of thought, he said, "Ah! I understand. Hashem's kindness may come in a form that I will be unable to recognize as kindness, and I may think it is something unkind. That is why I cannot delay expressing my thankfulness until then." After a few moments, R' Baruch began to cry. "How tragic it is! Hashem will be doing kindness with me, and I may be unable to recognize it!"

R' Eliyahu Dessler cites the Talmud stating that, except for the freedom to choose between right and wrong, good and evil, everything is decreed before one's birth, whether a person will be rich or poor, strong or weak, healthy or sickly (*Niddah* 30a). Why should a person be predestined to suffer, to be poor or sickly? R' Dessler answers that the Divine wisdom prescribes a *particular* mission for each *neshamah*. All *neshamos* are required to acknowledge the Oneness of Hashem; in order to achieve this, each *neshamah* must withstand trials in the form of challenges. For one *neshamah*, the challenge will be to accept poverty; for another *neshamah,* the challenge may be to resist the corruption brought on by wealth. For one *neshamah,* the challenge may be to accept physical suffering with trust in Hashem; for another, the challenge may be to withstand the urge to indulge in physicality. Only Hashem knows why different challenges are assigned to specific *neshamos.*

The Talmud says that a person is not culpable for feeling angry at Hashem when he is in agony (*Bava Basra* 16a). But if one will give some thought to the fact that he *does indeed* believe in Hashem, else he would not be angry at Him, he should contemplate about Hashem. Our belief is based on the revelation at Sinai, and the teachings conveyed to us by Moses, the prophets, and the Sages. Moses said, "You should know in your heart that just as a father will chastise his son, so Hashem, your G-d, chastises you" (*Deuteronomy* 8:5). "As a father is merciful toward his children, so Hashem shows mercy to those who fear Him" (*Psalms* 103:13). The mercy may sometimes be expressed in chastisement. Once a person realizes that Hashem is merciful, he can accept adversity with the faith that although we are unable to see it, the distress he experiences is somehow for his good. But to achieve this, one must know in his heart that Hashem relates to us like a loving father to his son. An intellectual understanding is not adequate. This is something one must believe in his heart. It was because *tzaddikim* had achieved this profound belief that they were able to accept *yissurim* with love.

R' Dessler stresses that the time to accept the concept that *yissurim* are essentially benevolent is when we are healthy and comfortable, because that is when we are free to contemplate on Divine *hashgachah*. Once we are in distress, we may be so preoccupied with our suffering that we are unable to ascribe to this tenet of faith (*Michtav M'Eliyahu* 3:237).

One can compare *yissurim* to the heat used to temper iron. Only after iron ore undergoes the intense heat of the forge can the finished metal withstand the stresses of the work to which it is put. Similarly, steel is formed through purification of the iron in the crucible in which the ore, at unbearably high temperature, becomes molten, after which it can be shaped into steel ingots. Thus, *yissurim* can be the catalyst that purifies the soul of the sufferer.

Yissurim cleanse a person and bring about forgiveness. We must understand that it is not because one has offended Hashem by sinning that he is assigned *yissurim* as a punishment. A sin is a stain on the *neshamah*, and *yissurim*, like a powerful detergent, remove the stain. If a person understands that he stands to profit by *yissurim*, he can have a positive attitude toward them.

R' Dessler says that if a person was told that he must remove people's shoes for them and put them on for them, he would feel degraded. However, the proprietor of a shoe store performs this action gladly and repeatedly, and he is not offended in the least. Why? Because that is how he makes his profit. Similarly, if one understands that *yissurim* are to his advantage, he may feel blessed in having them (*Michtav M'Eliyahu* 1:265).

In *Toras Avraham*, the ethicist R' Avraham Grodzinski presents a long essay on *yissurim*, pointing out that the chastisements of the prophets were meant to alert people to the fallacies in their concepts of *avodas Hashem*. There were generations in which people were formally observant of Torah, but did not recognize in what ways they were wrong. He cites as an example the generation of the Second Temple, who were fully observant of halachah, but were guilty of harboring unwarranted hatred in their hearts. Inasmuch as their physical actions were compatible with Torah, they did not realize the gravity of the sin of harboring hatred; the

Temple was destroyed and they were exiled to make them cognizant of this failure.

R' Grodzinski views *yissurim* as a wake-up call, in addition to being a cleansing process. *Yissurim* are intended to prompt soul-searching, and we should welcome *yissurim* just as we would appreciate being told that we were traveling in the wrong direction, away from our destination instead of toward it. *Mesillas Yesharim* gives an example of a person wandering in a maze, unable to find his way out. Atop a tall building another person can see all the paths in the maze, and he shouts to the wanderer, "Don't go on that path! It leads to nowhere. Follow my directions. They will lead you out of the maze." How foolish one would be to ignore this individual's directions and plod along on his own. How grateful one should be to be shown the correct path!

This, R' Grodzinski says, is the function of *yissurim.* "But," one might ask, "what am I doing that is so terribly wrong?" R' Grodzinski points out that the Jews of the generation of the Second Temple were *doing everything right.* Their exile was because of an improper *feeling.*

A person who suffers *yissurim* might say, "Am I so terrible a person that I should be subjected to such severe suffering?" The answer is, "No. To the contrary, you have *yissurim* because you are *good*, and the *yissurim* are to help you recognize flaws of which you may be unaware."

The example is given of two patients suffering from a malignant disease. One is beyond recovery, and there is no remedy that can cure him. The doctor prescribes medication to keep him as comfortable as possible. The other patient's condition is treatable. He may be put through procedures that are extremely uncomfortable. In contrast to the case of the first patient, the doctor's goal is cure rather than comfort.

How foolish this second patient would be to say, "Don't give me the treatment. Just keep me comfortable." This is why, R' Grodzinski says, we find that *tzaddikim* welcomed *yissurim*. They took these as a sign that Hashem is alerting them to improve themselves, because they are capable of being even better than they are.

We have no concept of Hashem's standards for *yissurim*. After the horrible massacres led by Chmielnicki in 1648, R' Yomtov Heller (author of *Tosafos Yom Tov* on the Mishnah), attributed the tragedy to the sin of talking in *shul* during prayers. There were people then who did not observe Torah at all, yet R' Heller placed the responsibility on whom? On Torah-observant people who attended *shul*! Unfortunately, we sometimes trivialize grave sins. The Torah says, "Accursed is one who strikes his fellow stealthily" (*Deuteronomy* 27:24); Rashi explains that this refers to one who speaks *lashon hara* about another person.

The Patriarch Abraham experienced a series of difficult challenges, and he and Sarah were childless until their advanced age. This was to refine them and elevate them to a level of spirituality that enabled them to be the progenitors of the Jewish People.

Acceptance of *yissurim* with the faith and trust in Hashem that these are ultimately to our own advantage is the true service of Hashem.

A WORD OF ADVICE:

Hashem loves us and every challenge we experience is for our own good. He does not subject one to yissurim as a punishment, but rather, the adversity is intended to remove the blight of sin or to spur the individual to greater spiritual heights.

20. EMUNAH IN DARKNESS

"The people stood from afar, and Moses approached the thick cloud where Hashem was" (*Exodus* 20:18).

Sometimes we feel that we are distanced from Hashem. We may feel Hashem's presence only in the brightness of the day. Moses approached the thick cloud. Moses knew that sometimes Hashem's presence is best felt in the darkness.

"It is good to thank Hashem and to sing praise to Your Name, O Exalted One; to relate Your kindness in the morning and Your faith in the nights" (*Psalms* 92:2-3). The authorship of this psalm is variously attributed to Moses and, according to the Midrash, to Adam. This theme is found in our prayers. In the morning we say, "Hashem, your G-d, is true, and certain, established and enduring, fair and faithful, beloved and cherished, delightful and pleasant." This we say in the brightness of the day, where Hashem's truth, fairness, and kindness can be seen by our mortal eyes. In the evening, however, we say, "Hashem, your G-d, is true, and all this is *emunah*." In moments of darkness, when we cannot see the kindness of Hashem, we know it exists because of our *emunah*.

"But," one may say, "it is so difficult to have firm *emunah* when one is experiencing severe adversity." Under severe stress, even the struggle to maintain *emunah* is meritorious. "Roam through the marketplaces of Jerusalem; see, know, and seek in its streets, if you find a person, if there is someone who does justice and seeks *emunah*, and I will forgive her" (*Jeremiah* 5:1). To *seek emunah*, to pursue faith, is praiseworthy.

Where should one look for *emunah*? Why, within oneself! It is there, but we may sometimes be unaware of it.

R' Shneur Zalman states in *Tanya* that during the Inquisition, when Jews were forced to renounce their faith in Hashem under threat of death, many Jews who were not at all observant of Torah chose to forfeit their lives rather than to deny Hashem. Inasmuch as they did not observe any of the mitzvos, what motivated them to give up their lives? It was because every Jew has a nucleus of *emunah*. Often a person's indulgence in earthly desires forms a thick shell around this nucleus, so that its presence is not recognized.

Diamonds lie in the earth for thousands of years, covered by layers of grime; when they are brought to the surface, one sees only a clump of earth, but when those layers of grime are removed and the stone is polished, the beautiful gem is exposed. We all have a nucleus of *emunah*, and when all goes well for us, we may not have reason to access it. It is when one experiences adversity and needs the *chizuk* of faith and trust in Hashem that he gropes for this concealed nucleus. As the Rebbe of Slonim says, "One must believe that he is a believer."

Moses said that when we are in distress, "From there you will seek Hashem, your G-d, and you will find Him, if you search for Him with all your heart and all your soul" (*Deuteronomy* 4:29). One of the commentaries points out that the latter part of this verse can also be translated, "if you search for Him *in* all your heart and all your soul." Our *emunah* is found within us. In keeping with the verse in *Jeremiah*, the Rebbe of Kotzk remarked, "'You will seek Hashem, and you will find Him' implies that the seeking *is* the finding."

In times of distress, some people recite Psalm 22, which states (v. 2), "My G-d, my G-d, why have You forsaken me?" and continues to discuss relying on G-d. In the weeks following the mourning of Tishah B'Av, we recite the *haftarah* from *Isaiah*

49:14-15, "Zion said, 'Hashem has forsaken me, My Lord has forgotten me.' Can a woman forget her nursling, withdraw from feeling compassion for the child of her womb? Even were these to forget, yet I will not forget you." Even when we are in profound distress, we should remember that Hashem's compassion for us far exceeds the most profound compassion a human can offer.

In his work on the mitzvos, Rambam says that the first mitzvah is to *believe* in Hashem, whereas in the Codex (*Yesodei HaTorah* 1:1), Rambam says that the foundation of Torah is to *know* that there is Hashem. There are two levels of *emunah*. We begin with belief, which is innate within our *neshamah*, but we must cultivate this belief so that we *know* it to be a fact.

We can cultivate and strengthen our *emunah* by reading the abundant Torah literature on *emunah* and the biographies of our *tzaddikim*. It is of utmost importance that we regularly recite the *Ani Maamin* (I Believe), the Thirteen Principles of *Emunah*. The Rebbe of Slonim says that recitation of *Ani Maamin* is not only an assertion of *emunah*, but also a prayer asking that Hashem help a person to strengthen his *emunah*.

A friend told me that he went to visit the Steipler Gaon. He knocked on the door, but there was no answer. The Steipler Gaon was hard of hearing, and had not heard the knock. My friend cautiously pushed the door open and entered. He saw that the Gaon was sitting without a *sefer*, whispering to himself. Inasmuch as he was not *davening*, my friend assumed the Steipler was reciting *Tehillim* (*Psalms*). He tiptoed behind him and heard the Gaon reciting the *Ani Maamin* and translating it into Yiddish, slowly repeating, "*Ani maamin, ich gloib* [I believe], etc."

Think of it! The great Gaon, who did not let a single moment pass without Torah study, felt that it was necessary to reinforce his *emunah*, and found the time not only to recite the *Ani Maamin* but also to translate it into Yiddish, to reinforce his understanding of it!

It is of interest that Ramban disagrees with Rambam. The Ramban maintains that while, of course, *emunah* is the foundation of *Yiddishkeit*, it cannot be considered a mitzvah, because a mitzvah, a commandment, presupposes that one knows that there is Someone Who issued that commandment; thus, *emunah* must *precede* mitzvos. The Rebbe of Slonim explains the Rambam's position: While the first level of *emunah*, belief in Hashem, cannot be considered a mitzvah, developing the *emunah* to its second level, to its becoming *knowledge*, a firm unshakable fact, constitutes the mitzvah of *emunah* (*Nesivos Shalom I*, 41-48).

> *A man told a rebbe all his troubles, and the rebbe said, "Hashem will help you."*

"But what will I do until Hashem helps me?" the man said.

The rebbe said, "Hashem said to Jacob, 'I will not forsake you until I have done what I have spoken for you' [Genesis 28:15]. Hashem will take care of you until He helps you."

It is precisely when one experiences adversity that one must make the effort to reinforce his *emunah*. The Rebbe of Slonim cites the Midrash stating that our ancestors were delivered from the bondage of Egypt by virtue of their *emunah*, and that the ultimate Redemption, too, will come by virtue of *emunah*. He adds that just as with the nation, so also with each individual; one will be delivered from personal travail by virtue of *emunah*.

A WORD OF ADVICE:

In times of travail, a firm unshakable emunah is a necessity. This emunah is found within oneself. Even in profound distress, we should remember that Hashem's compassion for us is immeasurable.

21. Is There a Silver Lining?

You may feel like closing this book, thinking, *This man must be crazy! I've lost my job, my stocks are worthless, I don't know how I'm to pay my mortgage, and he's talking about a silver lining!*

Here is a silver lining we may often fail to see.

Many years ago, in Jerusalem, I asked a tzaddik to pray for my brother, who was ill with cancer. As I left, the tzaddik said, "May you have many worries."

I was taken aback. "What kind of berachah is that?" I asked.

The tzaddik said, "It is impossible to go through life without any worries. If, G-d forbid, a person has a life-threatening problem, that obscures all his other worries, and he is totally occupied with this single very serious worry.

"At this time, you are consumed by only a single worry: your brother's serious illness; that concern has displaced all other worries. If you will have many worries, it will mean that none of them is so serious that it occupies your entire thinking. So my berachah is that you should have many worries."

In all likelihood, the economic crisis has caused you many worries. If you think of this, you will say, "Baruch Hashem."

That is a silver lining.

R' Samson Raphael Hirsch says that when two Hebrew words share similarities, it means that they are somehow topically related. How much more so when one word has two different meanings! The two meanings must be closely related.

The Hebrew word for *crisis* is *mashbeir* (shatter). *Mashbeir* is also the word for the obstetrical chair or birthing stool. More than just a few times, a personal crisis has led to the birth of something very positive.

The Talmud says that if the Torah had not been given to us, we would have been obligated to learn proper behavior from the observation of some animals (*Eruvin* 100b). I think that there is much we can learn from lobsters.

Have you ever thought about how a lobster grows? A lobster is a soft animal that lives within a rigid shell that cannot expand. How, then, can a lobster grow?

As the lobster grows, its shell becomes too confining and oppressive. Because it is uncomfortable, the lobster retreats to an underwater rock formation where it has some protection from predatory fish and sheds its shell. It then produces a new, more spacious shell. Eventually, this new shell becomes too confining, and the lobster repeats the process. It does so a number of times, until it reaches its maximum size.

The stimulus that enables the lobster to grow is *discomfort.* If lobsters had access to tranquilizers or painkillers, they would never grow!

What are we to learn from lobsters?

Comfort is not conducive to growth. Discomfort enables growth.

The lobster actually risks its life in order to grow, since, when it sheds its shell, it is defenseless against predatory fish.

"But," you may say, "who needs to grow? I'm perfectly satisfied with the way I am. I want to pay my bills. I want to be able to afford to educate my children. I want to be able to help support my married children. I'm not interested in growth."

I understand you perfectly. I am not one who can tolerate pain. When I have a toothache, I have only one thought: *I want relief!* That's where you are now. You are not interested in philosophical discussions or theological explanations. You want relief!

If there was any safe way of getting relief, I would wholeheartedly recommend it. We have already noted that escapist techniques, such as numbing oneself with alcohol or tranquilizers, are counterproductive. The fact is that there is no immediate relief. Of course you must consider every possible way to improve your situation. But let's not lose sight of the fact that this distress, this personal *mashbeir*, has the potential to give birth to something valuable.

Let us be honest with ourselves. When we were secure in our jobs and our investments were profitable, how much growing did we do?

What do I mean by *growing*? Personal growth depends on discovering what is truly important in life. We live by the words of the Torah, and say in the *berachah*, "… Who gave us a Torah of truth and implanted eternal life within us." What is this eternal life? In fact, what is our life all about?

When things go well, we may not stop to reflect on what we want to do with our lives. We may feel that what life is all about is what we do every day on the job or at the office or even at home. In *Light at the End of the Tunnel*, I wrote about a man who lived for his office. He had built up a huge financial empire, and all his thoughts and efforts went into the office.

When he went on vacation, he called the office several times a day. After he developed a serious health problem, however, his focus on life changed, and he realized that there were some things that surpassed even the office in importance.

The office is indeed important, but to the best of my knowledge, no one in the last phase of life has ever said, "My one regret is that I did not spend more time in the office." As we grow older, our perspective changes, and we may realize what the true values of life are.

Barry is a young man who consulted me at the insistence of his father, Stephen, who felt that since Barry was dropping out of law school, something must be wrong with him.

Stephen had been a very bright law student who fulfilled the class prediction that he would be the most likely to succeed. He developed a huge law firm and represented a number of major corporations. He was proud of his home and his luxury automobile.

Stephen's wife complained that he had no time for her or the children; he often spent late hours at the office and kept in frequent contact with the office when on vacation. "He lives for the firm, not for us," she complained. His wife was active in a number of community organizations, but he belittled her participation. His charity was essentially limited to the expected donation to the United Way.

Stephen's son, Barry, entered law school and did well. At the end of his second year, he shocked his parents by declaring that he was dropping out. Convinced that the young man must have had a mental crisis, they sent him to me for a psychiatric evaluation.

Barry was pleasant and completely coherent and appropriate in the interview. He denied feeling depressed. He said that while he initially had wanted to follow in his father's footsteps, he had begun rethinking this plan at the beginning of the second year in school.

"I know I could be a good lawyer," Barry said, "but I don't want to emulate my father. I respect him for his brilliance and accomplishments, but I can't see being the head of a large law firm as being a goal in life. I love my father, and I hate to say this, but all he is — is a lawyer, not really a person. I am not a particularly religious person, but I don't think that man was created only to perform at work. There has got to be something more to life.

"My dad is not a happy man. His preoccupation with the firm is his escape. A lot of his associates drink heavily, but he doesn't. The firm is his alcohol. When we're on vacation, he is in constant contact with the office. The office doesn't need him; he needs the office. His being away from the office is like a drunk running out of alcohol. I don't want to end up feeling miserable like my dad and looking for some kind of escape.

> *"I'm not sure what I'll do. I may even decide to go back to law school in the future, if they'll take me. Right now, I want to take some time off to find out what life is really all about and what I am all about. I have to find a goal that makes sense."*
>
> *I did not find anything wrong with Barry's mental status.*

One of the greatest books in all Torah literature is *Mesillas Yesharim*. The opening chapter is titled, "The duties of a person in the world." How often have we reflected on this? Have we even thought that we have a duty?

The Midrash says that after fleeing from Esau and being mistreated by Laban, the Patriarch Jacob wished to settle in tranquility, but G-d said, "Tranquility is in Gan Eden. In the earthly world, one must struggle" (*Bereishis Rabbah* 84:1). Although we may not understand why, it is evident that we are meant to struggle. When Jacob triumphed in his wrestling match with the angel, the latter said, "No longer will it be said that your name is Jacob, but Israel, for you have struggled (Hebrew: *sorisa*) with the Divine and with man and you triumphed (Hebrew: *vatuchal*) over them." If the point is that Jacob triumphed over the Divine and man, his name should have been *Michal*, which is derived from the word *vatuchal*. But the name *Yisrael* is related to *sorisa*: not to the triumph, but rather to the struggle.

Tanya and *Mesillas Yesharim*, each in its own way, state that man was put in this world to struggle, and it is a struggle that persists throughout one's lifetime.

Hashem created angels, holy spiritual beings. Angels were created in a state of completion. They do not have to grow spiritually. Hashem did not intend man to be just another angel. Rather, man was created with drives that are inimical to spirituality, and man is to subdue and channel these drives to become spiritual. Just as bodily muscles atrophy if they are not exercised, so, too, the human spirit withers if it is passive and tranquil. Man grows by struggling.

Yes, the shock of losing one's job and savings is enormous. It is difficult to imagine anything except, Heaven forbid, serious illness that is as shattering as sustaining these losses.

You know and I know that somehow we will survive this nightmare. Many people dismiss the thought of what their purpose in life is, because their belief that they do not have an ultimate purpose is too devastating. But what if our denial is ineffective and we are confronted with this question: Can we survive that?

Psalm 79 begins, "A song of Asaph: O G-d, the nations have entered into Your inheritance, they have defiled the Sanctuary of Your holiness, they have turned Jerusalem into heaps of rubble." The Midrash says, "Why is this psalm referred to as a '*song* of Asaph'? 'A *lamentation* of Asaph' would have been more appropriate, inasmuch as it speaks of the destruction of Jerusalem." The Midrash answers that the Jews of Jerusalem had been so sinful that the death penalty was warranted. Hashem commuted their sentence by destroying Jerusalem instead and sending the people into exile. That is why it deserves to be celebrated by song (*Eichah Rabbah* 4:15). In this horrible catastrophe, Asaph found a silver lining.

One can extrapolate this lesson to one's own experience. Of course, we have no way of knowing why this economic catastrophe has befallen so many of us. Nonetheless, contemplate the possibility that what we have perceived as a dreadful misfortune may indeed be a sign of Hashem's benevolence in sparing us from an even worse debacle.

You might not think of this as a silver lining, but because of the drastic changes in one's financial condition, the family may have to make some significant lifestyle changes. This should be discussed with the entire family: the parents and all the children. Yes, a 6-year-old should sit in on the session, because she, too, will be affected. Everyone should be helped to understand what happened to the economy, and that the job loss was not the fault of the father or the mother. There should be a frank discussion of some of the changes that this situation necessitates, such as concluding that not everyone will be able to attend cousin Shimmie's bar mitzvah celebration at the Kosel next year, as had been planned. Birthday gifts will be smaller (and probably more sensible) and we're not sure about the situation regarding summer camps. This is a time when the family must pull together to overcome hardships and cope with the disappointments, with a minimum of discomfort. The children should be encouraged to ask questions, and the best possible explanations should be given. Stick to the facts and don't frighten youngsters by presenting worst-case scenarios that most probably will never arise; young children cannot always differentiate between supposition and reality. The session should end with much embracing. Family support is one of the most effective methods for stress reduction.

Why does this situation constitute a silver lining? Because it may be the first time that the whole family has ever come together for a serious discussion and recognized that the whole family is a unit in which everyone is affected. It may be the first time that all the family members hear, "We're in this together and we must pull together." This is a life lesson that will serve every member of the family well.

Indeed, the fact that the family may have to adopt a more frugal lifestyle may itself be a silver lining. We live in an era of "entitlement." Everyone feels that he or she is entitled to the niceties in life. More than a few youngsters have turned to addictive behavior because they feel that they have not received the pleasure to which they are entitled. Living a more frugal lifestyle sends the message that one cannot have everything one wants and to which one is "entitled." J.C. Penny was asked the secret of his success. He said, "Adversity. I would never have amounted to anything had I not been forced to come up the hard way."

The Steipler Gaon said, "When we were children, we were satisfied with the bare necessities of survival. A fresh apple was a rare treat, and candy was almost unheard of. The "new suit" received for Pesach was either a hand-me-down or something which Mother had somehow ingeniously refashioned. Today's children are given so much that if they do not get something they want, it is a tragedy."

The family pulling together to cope with the crisis brings to mind the unfortunate fact that sometimes it is only a sad event that brings a family together. It is not too unusual for there to be such bad feelings among siblings that when there is a family *simchah* one sibling may say, "If this brother/sister will be there, I will not come. You can invite me or him/her, but not both of us." Yet, if there is, G-d forbid, a funeral, everyone comes. It is high time that this insanity comes to an end. Family *simchos* should be shared by all family members.

Obviously, it is bad to fall, but if one has fallen, one may sometimes see something valuable on the ground that one could not see when upright; however, this will only happen if one looks around.

I'd like to share a story about a patient who sustained a shoulder fracture in an car accident. The nerves from the spinal cord to the right arm were severed, and she had no sensation in or motion of that arm. The surgeon performed a nerve repair, attaching the proximal to the distal end of the nerve. However, unless nerve fibers would grow down the channels, attaching the nerve ends accomplished nothing. She was told that it would be months before the outcome of the nerve repair was known. Her arm was put into a sling, and she had no way of knowing if she would ever regain the use of her right arm.

After several months, she was playing cards and smoking a cigarette, holding both in her left hand. As she manipulated the cards, the cigarette fell onto her right hand and she felt the sting of the burn. She threw the cards into the air and jumped for joy, shouting "I'm hurting! I'm hurting!"

Usually, we are unhappy when we feel pain. To this woman, the pain was an indication that the nerve fibers had grown along the channels and she would regain the use of her right arm. She welcomed the pain.

As I write this, I am experiencing pain in parts of my body that I never even knew I had, but I am happy. Let me explain.

Several years ago, my brother fell down a flight of stairs and fractured his cervical spine. Due to the fracture, he stopped breathing, and the loss of oxygen caused brain damage, He was resuscitated, but was totally paralyzed from the neck down. He lingered for almost a year.

Just two days ago, I fell down a flight of stairs, stricking my neck, but Hashem spared me. I said Bircas Hagomel today, thanking Hashem for His great chesed. If not for Hashem's chesed, I would have suffered the same fate as my brother.

I have some pain medication, but I do not take it. Each time I feel pain, I am reminded of my fall and how near I was to utter disaster; I realize that only the chesed of Hashem saved me, and I recite the verse of Hodu, "Give thanks to Hashem for He is good; for His kindness endures forever" (Psalms 118:1). It is so easy to forget Hashem's chesed. I don't want to forget. I actually welcome the pain. For the first time, I can understand the concept of yissurim besimchah, accepting suffering with joy.

A WORD OF ADVICE: *A personal crisis is often the catalyst for the birth of something positive. If we take the time to make the effort, we will invariably find the silver lining in the cloud of these stormy times.*

APPENDIX:

STRESS-REDUCTION SUGGESTIONS

Yes, I know. Securing a job and increasing the value of your investments is a surefire way of reducing your stress, and I sincerely hope that comes about soon. However, until then, it is important to find ways to reduce the consequences of the stress. Not only are the consequences of excessive, constant stress damaging both physically and psychologically, but they can also stand in the way of improving your circumstances.

I've already pointed out that tranquilizers are *not* the way to go. The more of the following suggestions you implement, the better the results of stress reduction will be.

∽ EXERCISE ∽

Everyone knows that exercise is good for you. Exercise strengthens the heart, expands lung capacity, increases muscles strength and builds bone, burns fat, and improves the function of the immune system.

Many studies have confirmed that exercise is mood lifting, probably by raising the levels of endorphins (the brain's own opiates) and the neurotransmitters norepinephrine and serotonin. People who exercise regularly are better able to cope with stressful events.

Exercising facilitates weight loss and helps maintain a healthy weight. Building muscle helps to reduce fat.. Exercise can also forestall some of the diseases common to aging and may prevent or delay mental slowing.

Aerobic exercises include brisk walking (you might strap on an iPod or a portable MP3 player to make the time fly). Cycling, rowing, treadmill, swimming, and racket sports are exercises you can do even without joining a gym. Of course, joining a gym provides structure and access to more sophisticated equipment. If you can, exercise together with a friend; the companionship helps keep you motivated. Check with your doctor as to how much exercise you should be doing.

∾ Calming Techniques ∾

There are a number of techniques that can provide safe, constructive relaxation.

The Relaxation Response, by Dr. Herbert Benson, documents the value of progressive muscle relaxation, breathing exercises, meditation, and visualization. Study after study has shown the effectiveness of these relaxation methods in reducing chronic pain, lowering blood pressure, and improving other stress-related conditions.

I have mentioned the book, *Jewish Meditation — A Practical Guide,* by Rabbi Aryeh Kaplan. I strongly urge you to get this book and follow its directions. You will need to be patient, since we are not used to meditating, and both time and practice are necessary to master the techniques, but the results are well worth the investment. In all likelihood, you have been living at a frenetic pace, and sitting quietly, concentrating on your breathing, is just about the last thing on your agenda. But make no mistake about it: untreated stress can take a heavy toll.

People are prone to dismiss these techniques because they do not seem sufficiently scientific. This is reminiscent of the story of Naaman, general of the army of the king of Aram, who suffered from *tzaraas*, a leprouslike skin condition (*II Kings* 5:1-14). Having heard of the wonders performed by the prophet Elisha, Naaman came to him to be healed. When Elisha told him to bathe in the Jordan River, Naaman became enraged. He had expected the prophet to perform some mysterious ritual, and he said that the rivers in Aram were just as good as the Jordan. At the advice of his servants, he consented to bathe in the Jordan, and was completely healed.

Do not dismiss meditation because it is not dramatic enough to be effective. Be patient and persistent, and you will benefit greatly.

Visualization is a variant of meditation, during which you concentrate your mind on a particular image, perhaps a relaxing experience that you had or can fantasize. If your mind wanders from the scene, you refocus. Eventually you will be able to maintain a relaxing image. Audiotapes and CD's on guided imagery are available to help you visualize.

Biofeedback is a relaxation method utilizing electronic signals to help your body learn how to relax. It does so by measuring skin temperature and/or muscle tension. The signals inform you when your body is relaxing, and in a number of sessions (12 on the average), your body learns what it must do to relax. In addition to reducing anxiety, biofeedback can be very helpful in treating both migraine and muscle-tension headaches as well as back pain. Your physician can provide a referral to a biofeedback therapist.

∽ ART, GARDENING, AND HOBBIES ∾

You haven't thought of yourself as an artist? Well, even if you will never be a Rembrandt, you may be surprised at what you can create. Simply standing before an easel and experimenting with colors and shapes, taking a class, or working with any artistic medium can help reduce stress and help you focus on the positive elements in your life.

Tending a garden can be fun, whether one is cultivating flowers or vegetables. By the time a tomato is full grown, bursting with color and flavor, and ready for eating, you may have invested many hours and considerable energy, but watching it grow and nursing it along can be very relaxing. This is also true of flowers, which can enrich your life as they add color and fragrance to your home.

∽ EATING ∽

While eating is primarily intended to provide the body with the nutrients it needs, emotions are very intertwined with eating. Some people react to stress by not eating, others by overeating.

In the acute stress of the fight-or-flight reaction, one does not think of food. When running away from a tiger or escaping from a burning building, one does not stop for a sandwich. The adrenaline that is released in the fight-or-flight reaction actually suppresses appetite, but when the acute phase is over, the body secretes glucocorticoids that can increase appetite.

Some types of foods appear to have a more tranquilizing effect than others. If you're uptight because of a final exam, you are much more likely to reach for chocolate or cookies than for a stalk of celery. Perhaps the body wants an immediate source of sugar to provide energy to cope with stress. So we get a "rush" with carbohydrates, but when the rush recedes, we are likely to feel a plunge, and then, you know what: we go for more carbohydrates. That starts the vicious cycle that results in unwanted weight gain that in and of itself generates stress.

Caffeine is not a tranquilizer. To the contrary, caffeine is a stimulant, and it can, therefore, give one a feeling of recharged energy. However, this "lift" is short lived, and may be followed by a feeling of fatigue, which may result in recourse to more caffeine. "Caffeinism" is a real condition, and addiction to caffeine is quite difficult to overcome, because lowering the intake may cause severe headache. Caffeine may raise the level of adrenaline, resulting in the jitters, heart palpitations, elevated blood pressure, and insomnia.

Coffee is not the only source of caffeine. Many soft drinks have caffeine, and a "chocaholic" may also ingest a considerable amount of caffeine. It is wise not to exceed four cups of coffee a day, or the equivalent in caffeinated soft drinks. As an alternative, try herbal tea blends that do not contain caffeine and can be very soothing.

Many people feel that smoking cigarettes is relaxing, and that cannot be denied. However, you would be better off numbing yourself by hitting yourself over the head with a sledgehammer, which will not lead to lung cancer, emphysema, and heart disease. If you're hooked on cigarettes, there are programs to help you overcome that addiction.

You might be surprised to know that drinking adequate amounts of water can help relieve stress. Often people are actually dehydrated, yet they are totally unaware of it. Dehydration can cause irritability, fatigue, headaches, and muddled thinking. You might say, "I don't feel thirsty." By the time you feel thirsty, your dehydration is advanced. Incidentally, caffeine and alcohol aggravate dehydration. It is recommended that you drink two liters (eight glasses) of water every day.

More about eating. It's not only what you eat, but also *how* you eat. Mealtime should be relaxing. Don't talk business during mealtime and don't check your computer, and for heaven's sake, don't look at the stock-market report! If you're eating alone, read the comics page or the sports column. Leave the news for later.

A study was done to see if it was possible to identify why some families experienced difficulties while parenting their adolescents while others did not. Hundreds of families were interviewed and tons of data were fed into computers. The only significant factor was that in the happier families, the family shared meals more often. A pleasant mealtime can be a stress reducer for everyone in the family.

If you want to lose weight, avoid "crash" diets. It never ceases to amaze me that, every month, at least five "miracle diets" are on the magazine covers. It should be common knowledge that you may indeed lose 30 pounds quite quickly with a miracle diet, but you are virtually certain to bounce back by gaining 40 pounds.

It's a good idea to consult a dietitian for a well-balanced diet. Every hospital has a dietitian on staff, and in a brief interview you can be given information on a healthy diet. Whole grains are rich sources of fiber and have been shown to lower cholesterol. Stay away from sugary or corn syrup-laden treats. It's best to avoid packaged snack foods.

What about food supplements, such as vitamins, minerals, and herbs? Check with your doctors. There are vitamins that can be harmful if taken in excessive amounts or in conjunction with prescribed medications.

∾ SLEEP ∾

Sleep is when the body does most of its rebuilding. Insufficient sleep can make one groggy during the day and befuddle one's thinking and memory. When you are well rested, you can cope much better, whereas if you are sleep-deprived, molehills may become mountains. During sleep, the body's stress hormones are reduced, whereas with sleep deprivation, these hormones may increase, resulting in a vicious cycle. Stress causes loss of sleep, which causes more stress, which results in more loss of sleep, etc.

I've already stated that except for infrequent, brief intervals, sleep medications may cause more problems than they solve.

A warm bath can help you relax. Soft, soothing music or "white noise" that has repetitive rhythms can induce sleep. A glass of warm milk is a safe sedative, because it contains L-tryptophane, a relaxing amino acid. Some herbal teas, such as chamomile, are relaxing. Check out aromatherapy; some fragrances can reduce tension and are safe tranquilizers.

The amount of sleep necessary varies with individuals. In general, a person requires seven to eight hours. Your bedroom should be an oasis of tranquility; install soft lighting, read a book, or play restful music to induce calm and a good night's sleep, rather than play computer games or text friends.

These are just some highlights about stress reduction. You can find more details in books on stress and individualize a stress reduction that is most suitable for you.

One last thought. The prayer used at AA meetings can be very helpful to everyone, not simply to addictive personalities. The prayer requests, "G-d grant me the serenity to accept the things I cannot change, the courage to change the things I can, and the wisdom to know the difference."

It is only logical. What else can you do about things you cannot change other than to accept them? Accepting them does not mean you approve of them. It just means, "Don't deny reality." If there are things that can be changed for the better, take courage and do not miss the opportunity to improve your life.

And what is the wisdom? The wisdom is to know that what is always changeable is *oneself*, but it may take courage to make changes in oneself. To weather the storms of life, we must change our outlook, recognize that Hashem loves us and is not punishing us, and have faith that all He does is for the best.